intro

Hello!

It's said there's a book in each of us. That's probably true, even if it's only your life story. The trouble is, getting it published... or it was.

Amazon now sells more digital books than anything else, which is great news for all aspiring writers and budding publishers. By cutting out the costly, ponderous cycle of printing and distributing your work, you can also cut out a whole industry of publishers, editors and marketing agents.

With some inexpensive tools and little bit of know-how – which we'll provide in this guide – you, too, can set yourself up a digital publisher. We'll walk you through every step involved in writing, formatting and selling your book through the biggest online bookstores.

We would say 'good luck', but in truth you no longer need it!

Nik Rawlinson

locations 3 – 12

100%

How to Publish your own eBook

WRITTEN BY Nik Rawlinson *www.nikrawlinson.com*

ADVERTISING
MAGBOOK ACCOUNT MANAGER Katie Wood 07971 937162
SENIOR MAGBOOK EXECUTIVE Matt Wakefield 020 7907 6617
DIGITAL PRODUCTION MANAGER Nicky Baker 020 8907 6056

DENNIS PUBLISHING LTD
GROUP MANAGING DIRECTOR Ian Westwood
MANAGING DIRECTOR John Garewal
MD OF ADVERTISING Julian Lloyd-Evans
NEWSTRADE DIRECTOR David Barker
CHIEF OPERATING OFFICER Brett Reynolds
GROUP FINANCE DIRECTOR Ian Leggett
CHIEF EXECUTIVE James Tye
CHAIRMAN Felix Dennis

PUBLISHING AND MARKETING
MAGBOOK PUBLISHER Dharmesh Mistry 020 7907 6100
MARKETING EXECUTIVE Paul Goodhead 020 7907 6012

LICENSING AND REPRINTS
Material in *Publish your own eBook* may not be reproduced in any form
without the publisher's written permission. It is available for licensing overseas.
For details about licensing contact Carlotta Serantoni,
+44 (0) 20 7907 6550, *carlotta_serantoni@dennis.co.uk*
To syndicate this content, contact Anj Dosaj-Halai,
+44 (2)20 7907 6132, *anj_dosaj-halai@dennis.co.uk*

MAGBOOK

The 'MagBook' brand is a trademark of
Dennis Publishing Ltd, 30 Cleveland Street,
London W1T 4JD. Company registered in
England. All material © Dennis Publishing
Ltd, licensed by Felden 2012, and may not be
reproduced in whole or part without the consent
of the publishers. *How to Publish your own eBook* is
an independent publication. All trademarks are the
properties of their respective owners.

Printed in England by BGP Print Ltd,
Chaucer International Estate, Launton Road,
Bicester OX6 7QZ

Contents

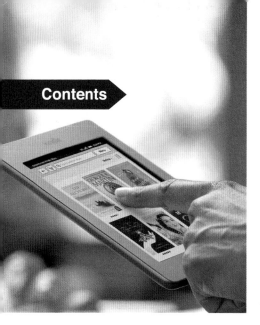

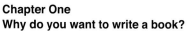

Chapter One

Why do you want to write a book?

Is a book the best format for your content?

In this chapter

Alternatives to book publishing
- Plain text
- Portable Document Format
- App
- Web site
- Magazine or printed book

eBook
eBook formats

There's something special about producing a book. The months – years, sometimes – of effort involved in putting one together are more than repaid by the warm glow that comes from holding the finished product in your hands. Even if you never sell a single copy, it's undeniable that there's something special about joining such auspicious ranks as those that count Dickens, Austen and the Brontes among their number.

But ask yourself: what is it you really want? What's your motivation in setting out on the long, hard but ultimately rewarding journey that takes you from blank page to written book? If it's the burning desire to tell a story – whether fiction or fact – that you've promised to write for years, or a need to prove to yourself once and for all that there really is a book in each and every one of us, then welcome along. You've come to the right place.

If, on the other hand, all you want is to see your name on the spine of a printed book, then think again.

The worlds of books and publishing are undergoing a revolution more dramatic than any it's seen in the last 500 years. Paper and print are losing the battle with pixels and screens as more and more readers drop dead-tree products in favour of eco-friendly downloads. It's less about the medium now, and more about the story. Ever more books are being sold on the merits of their content, as they no longer have a physical form.

For the purposes of this guide, we'll continue to refer to your written, published work as a 'book'. You may prefer 'eBook', 'download' or simply 'file', but over time this will become about as relevant to the medium that holds your written work as 'horseless carriage' is to car.

It's true that the Shorter Oxford English Dictionary defines a book as a 'collection of sheets of paper or other material, blank, written, or printed, fastened together so as to form a material whole,' but that particular entry appears third in its list of possible definitions. Two spots above it sits 'Book: a writing, a written document; a charter, a deed.'

What, then, is your published digital download if not a book?

Before you get on with the task of producing such a document, though, you must answer one key question: is a book the most appropriate medium for your content, or might your subject be better served by something else?

Alternatives to publishing a book

There's never been a wider choice of formats in which to publish your work. The almost universal availability of reliable, fast, permanent Internet connections means it's easy for any – and indeed all – of us to publish our work. And we can do so with close to 100% certainty that it'll be read by at least a small, and potentially huge, audience.

Better yet, as you have ultimate control over the medium, you don't need to jump through publishers' restrictive hoops to produce something that they're interested in selling. Instead you can write what interests you and your defined audience, whatever its size.

Plain text is a great choice for newsletter publishing as it can be read on any platform, from an ereader to a humble email application. However, formatting choices are slim and it makes no provision for copy protection.

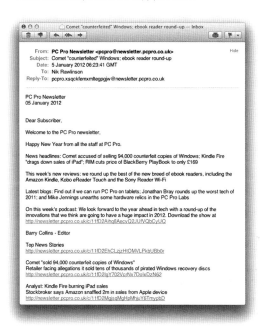

Plain text

By far the simplest and most reliable format for your work is a plain text file. This format has been relied upon for decades by publishers of online newsletters and fan sites. All leading ereading hardware can process text files, so whatever device your audience reader has bought, you can be sure they'll be able to access your work. Better yet, they don't actually need an ereader at all, as plain text can just as easily be rendered on a regular computer in a discrete file, or the body of an email.

However, for some the very simplicity of plain text introduces more problems than it solves.

For starters, your formatting options are seriously limited. When we say plain text we mean just that: the lowest common denominator. We aren't talking about a Word or RTF file in which you could use tables and columns, different font faces and sizes.

We mean plain ASCII text with double carriage returns to mark out sections, dashes used to underline headings and stars or dots for bullet points. Go any further than this and you can't be sure that what you send to your readers will look the same on their screen as it does on yours.

More critically, though, for anyone who wants to make a living from digital self-publishing, is the lower regard with which your readers will hold a plain text product. No matter how long it took you to write your book, or how much research was involved, the perceived value of a plain text presentation will also be lower than almost any other. Only handwritten notes on scraps of paper come lower down the chain. Unless you're giving away your work for free, we'd therefore recommend steering clear of plain text wherever possible, as even the most basic improvements in presentation, such as using a word processor to tweak the layout and then printing it as a PDF (see below), will increase the price you can legitimately hope to achieve when you put it on sale.

Perhaps the most serious limitation of plain text, though, is the lack of any kind of copy protection. It is the ultimate open format, and easily copied and distributed without your authorisation. While no format is immune to piracy, plain text offers you no protection at all, which only reinforces our assertion that unless you're willing to give away your work, and distribution is more important to you than profits, plain text is a format best avoided.

PDF is the format of choice for sending magazines to printers, and a reliable option for publishers who want what their readers see (*above*) to be a close approximation of their original layouts (*left*).

Portable Document Format (PDF)

PDF first appeared in 1993. Initially a proprietary format developed by Adobe, it became an open standard in 2008. It's long been the dominant production format in the professional publishing industry, as it has consistently proved itself to be a reliable means of transmitting laid-out pages to printers without their formatting being mangled in the process. This gives publishers themselves a high degree of confidence that what gets printed will closely mirror what they originally laid out in their desktop publishing application.

You might expect that, as we traverse a transitional phase in which the printed word is becoming less important, we would also see the slow demise of traditionally print-focused technologies such as PDF, but that's not the case at all. PDF is just as important when it comes to presenting information online as it is in print. Everything from instruction manuals to club newsletters are being published in digital-only format using PDF and rendered either in Adobe's own Reader application, or various third-party tools.

As with plain text, the cost of entry is low for anyone looking to use this as their preferred publishing format, as many consumer tools include a built-in PDF export option, while Mac users benefit from having the format built into the very core of their operating system.

However, many of these output tools remain simplistic when compared to Adobe's own Acrobat Pro application, which allows you to tweak the content of a compiled PDF document and apply a degree of rights restrictions to protect your work and potential income. This includes protecting the file so that it can only be opened by those who have paid you for a password, and preventing your customers printing the file.

Although PDF is a secure format, bear in mind that as soon as you've sold the password to a protected file to your first customer there's little beyond guilt and high moral standards to stop them passing it on to others, either for free or by reselling it. Formatting and distributing your book as a protected PDF file therefore offers only basic protection from misuse by nefarious readers.

App

The explosive growth of tablet computers – in particular the Apple iPad and Amazon Kindle Fire – has been matched only by the growth of applications (usually abbreviated to 'App') to run on them.

The most notable among these are games such as Cut the Rope and Angry Birds, which have sold in their millions, but look closer and you'll find a growing selection of revolutionary books, too.

Chief among these is Al Gore's *Our Choice*. Produced by Push Pop Press, which has since been acquired by Facebook, it set out to 'change the way we read books', and few would argue that it has done anything but succeed. *Our Choice* is like no other book you'll have read, fully embracing the opportunities delivered by the new media of pixels and multi-touch displays.

As well as regular flowing text and static images, *Our Choice* is packed with moving graphics, video, images you can touch and twist, and audio files that together tell its story using whatever method is most appropriate to the part of the book you have open at the time.

However, the barriers to entry here are high. You can't sit down on a Monday morning to format your content this way and expect to be finished by Friday afternoon, as you can with a regular eBook. Instead you need videographers, coders, sound recorders and someone who can navigate your book's passage through the approval process inherent in publishing it on a third-party tablet platform.

In short, you need a team. If you have one, then accept our sincere congratulations, but be aware that this book isn't aimed at someone with your level of resources at their disposal.

Website

A website offers many of the advantages of a book and an app combined while also suffering from some of the problems that inflict those who choose plain text or PDF as their output medium. While it's a quick and easy way to get your content online, even traditional publishers are finding it difficult to turn some of the world's biggest web properties into profitable products.

Counting in web publishing's favour are the ability to easily split your book into logical chapters simply by starting a new file and lacing them together using hyperlinks.

Al Gore's *Our Choice* makes the most of the platform on which it is published – the iPad – with audio, video, and animated graphics. This order of publishing is resource-intensive and beyond the reach of most eBook authors.

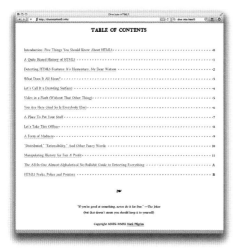

Mark Pilgrim's *Dive Into HTML5* is published both as a book and a website. This replicates the content of the book, split into clear chapters laced together by the hyperlinked index.

Further, with the accelerating adoption of HTML5 you can now embed a wider range of live media formats, including both video and audio, with a great deal of confidence as fewer of your readers will need to install a plug-in to view them.

However, content protection is notoriously weak, as even a so-called paywall, which requires use of a password or browser cookies to restrict your content only to those who have paid for access, won't stop them from copying words and images wherever they like.

Unless you want to follow Pilgrim's example and make your content freely available alongside your commercial product, a website is therefore better used as a sales tool for your book. Include generous samples to whet potential readers' appetites and induce a sale, but be sure not to give away the crown jewels. Allude to the juiciest sections of your work without revealing the punchline.

Magazine or printed book

There's a good reason that most people who work in the magazine and book publishing industries are mere employees and not owners: expense and complexity. Publishing is notoriously resource-intensive, requiring considerable reserves to produce, publish and successfully market a product. For this reason it takes a long time to get started and, more often than not, even longer to apply the brakes when it starts to go wrong.

As Felix Dennis, owner of Dennis Publishing and some of the UK's biggest magazine brands, put it in his book *How to Get Rich*:

> Let us say a dying magazine [losing $3m a year] has a million subscribers. Most of them are not 'real' subscribers [because they only subscribed to get their hands on a free gift], but, even so, they have paid their dollar per copy and are owed, on average, six more issues. This means the cost of reimbursing the subscribers alone will exceed $6 million in refunds.
>
> Of course, the publisher will also face other closure costs, including redundancy payments to magazine staff, rebates to advertisers and possibly to printers and paper merchants and a

host of other creepy-crawlies that will come slithering out of the woodwork when news that the ship is sinking spreads abroad. In all, sudden-death closure costs might be as high as $8 million.

The publisher's only hope is to cut costs to the bone, cease soliciting any discounted subscriptions, fulfil the subscriptions with very thin, very cheap editions of the magazine... and thereby reduce what, in the jargon, we call the 'subs liability'... In the meantime, the publishers hope that many staff will not wait to be fired but will seek other jobs and reduce closure costs by reducing redundancy payments. It took one of the largest magazine-publishing corporations in America over five years to bring about the closure of what was then still one of the best-known magazines in the world...

Over five years, in our hypothetical example, losses would be over $15 million – surely more than the cost of instantly shooting the brute? Yes, but that $15 million will have been spread out over those five years. The parent company can afford to carry such a burden. Profits will only be slightly affected each year and senior executives will still receive their precious annual bonuses. Even better, the share price will suffer mildly, if at all. On the other hand, if the full $8 million (or more) for sudden death was charged in a single year, not only would the senior management's bonuses evaporate... the share price would probably take a hit from negative publicity and profit-and-loss considerations.

You may think we're getting ahead of ourselves talking about bonuses and share prices, but many of the factors that affect the profitability of a major publisher should form part of your considerations, too. Do you have the resources to start up a print and publish operation? More to the point, do you have the time?

Digital publishing cuts the turnaround time involved in coming up with a saleable idea, writing it and getting it into a format in which you can market it from months to weeks – and in some cases days.

eBook

An eBook, then, offers the best of all worlds. It's quick and easy to produce, and requires little in the way of specialised equipment. You can produce one on your own, without the help of a large team, and you don't need the resources and expertise involved in producing a app. Neither need you put aside the amount of time required to turn out a printed book or magazine, however tempting it may be to produce something physical that you can hold in your hand.

eBook formats

If you're certain that an eBook is the most appropriate format for your content, you need to settle on a format. Our advice is to publish in as many formats as possible to maximise the chances your audience will be able to access your work.

The two leading formats are ePub, which many consider to be an open industry standard, and Mobipocket. While ePub is compatible with almost every ereader available, including the iPad's iBooks app, and the hardware readers from Kobo and Sony, Amazon favours Mobipocket and uses it as the basis of the protected books it sells for its Kindle readers and apps.

Amazon can handle the conversion from ePub to Mobipocket when you add your compiled book to its catalogue, but it makes more sense to perform the conversion yourself if at all possible. In this way you can conduct a final quality control inspection to ensure it meets the high standards you would expect of any book you pay for and download yourself.

In chapter three, we'll show you how to produce books for both formats. First, though, we'll take a look at how you can write a successful book.

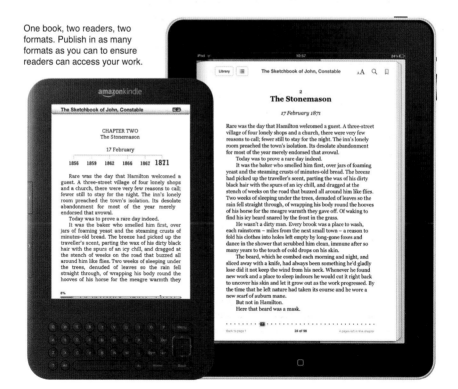

One book, two readers, two formats. Publish in as many formats as you can to ensure readers can access your work.

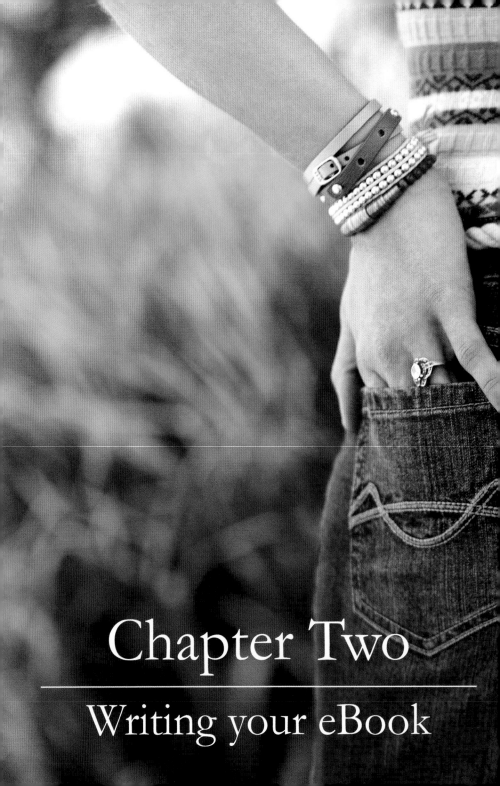

Chapter Two

Writing your eBook

What kind of book do you want to write?

It goes without saying that for any book to be successful, it has to be one that people want to read. That's as true for a factual book that someone is forced to plough through for their work or study as it is for pulp fiction and great literature.

So, how do you go about structuring a book to ensure it has the best chance of hitting the bestseller lists? It starts with the very first word. That's where you must you grab your reader's attention, and then hold it until your final full stop through a mixture of compelling writing and careful, well-considered structure.

In this chapter

Structuring your book
Writing fiction
Writing non-fiction
Images
- A picture costs a thousand words...
- Compression
- Colour
- Image size
Embedding images

Writing fiction

In his book *The 38 Most Common Fiction Writing Mistakes (and how to avoid them)* – one of the most useful books a first-time writer could ever hope to read – Jack M Bickham turns his mind back to childhood, and the cold mornings he spent sitting in his father's Buick as it ticked over in the garage, while he waited for the engine to warm up.

> In those days it was considered good form to warm your engine before driving the car. Multiviscosity engine oil was far in the future, and the theory was that the motor should idle a while under no strain while the heat of ignition warmed the oil so it could circulate more freely, providing better lubrication.
>
> Those days are long gone. But, amazingly, fiction writers still do the same kind of unnecessary and wasteful thing in starting their stories...
>
> Readers today – and that of course includes editors who will buy or reject your work – are more impatient than ever before. They will not abide a story that begins with the author warming his engines. If a setting needs to be described, it can be described later, after you have gotten the story started. If background must be given the reader, it can be given later, after you have intrigued him with the present action of the story.

Bickham's advice was published in 1992, 15 years before the first Kindle arrived, yet it has ever greater currency today than it did back then.

Each of the major online eBook retailers lets your potential audience download a sample of your book – often between 5% and 10% of your opening pages – that they can try before deciding whether they want to buy the complete product. It's the digital equivalent of leafing through a physical book in your high-street bookshop. If you want your readers to go ahead and spend real money on your book, it's essential that by the time they get to the end of the sample they're itching to discover what happens next.

Achieving this is a three-part formula: one part good writing, one part hitting the ground running (follow Bickham's engine advice) and one part intrigue. Why would your readers buy your book if they can already guess the ending by the time they've got to the last screen of your sample? They won't be hungry for answers; instead they'll be bored and uninspired and perhaps feel slightly cheated. Either way, they certainly won't be clicking 'buy now'.

Strive to create an air of intrigue and mystery, but avoid leading your readers up too many blind alleys or keeping important information from them any longer than you need. Drop hints and give them clues throughout so that by the time you reveal your murderer, unmask your blackmailer or spin the twist at the end of your tail they're kicking

One of fiction's greatest openings is paragraph one, page one of George Orwell's *1984*, which throws the reader into an unfamiliar world of which they can't help but wish to discover more.

Nineteen Eighty-Four

Part I

Chapter I

It was a bright cold day in April, and the clocks were striking thirteen. Winston Smith, his chin nuzzled into his breast in an effort to escape the vile wind, slipped quickly through the glass doors of Victory Mansions, though not quickly enough to prevent a swirl of gritty dust from entering along with him.

The hallway smelt of boiled cabbage and old rag mats. At one end of it a coloured poster, too large for indoor display, had been tacked to the wall. It depicted simply an enormous face, more than a metre wide: the face of a man of about forty-five, with a heavy black moustache and ruggedly handsome features. Winston made for the stairs. It was no use trying the lift. Even at the best of themselves for not having seen it coming themselves.

There's no intrigue in secrets, only in hints, and few will be satisfied when you introduce a new character on page 390 out of 400 as the evil mastermind whose actions were described throughout the book, but whose presence was never felt.

Readers want to see characters develop, and we all enjoy the thrill of the chase. It's far more satisfying wondering who dealt a fatal blow when it could only ever have been one of the characters laced through your book.

Drip-feed your readers all the hints they need to work out the end of your story themselves, but take care not to invoke a premature denouement.

Writing non-fiction

Fiction is, for most people, the Holy Grail of written creative work. Tell people you're a writer and with very few exceptions they'll be enthusiastic and interested... right up until the point you tell them your latest work was a treatise on European integration and its effect on biodiversity in bovine herds in Central and Eastern Europe.

Those exceptions are the people at whom your book is aimed: those for whom bovine biodiversity is a hook on which much of their professional or (less likely) personal lives hang. In the same way that a fiction writer strives to keep their audience engaged as their story progresses, so you need to keep the farmers, policy makers and researchers clicking back and forth through your eBook engrossed, enthralled and hungry for more.

What you must not do, though, is leave them wondering what comes next.

While a successful work of fiction must keep its readers guessing, a work of non-fiction must guide them by the hand. Keep in mind that most of your readers will be looking for particular information and will likely need to identify specific sections quickly and easily, either right away or at some point in the future.

It's therefore even more important in non-fiction that you clearly signpost what's coming next and how what you're writing right now relates to the rest of your work.

Careful and judicious use of cross-headings to mark out minor changes in subject, and chapter breaks to corral larger sections, help your readers quickly isolate the very section they need at any point.

However, don't assume that your reader will consume your book piecemeal. While it's true that reference works such as the Haynes series of car manuals, Mrs Beeton's Book of Household Management and even this guide to some degree

Consistent use of chapter breaks and cross-headings will help your readers to navigate the various sections of a non-fiction book.

will serve as a dip-in, dip-out product (after all, it's unlikely that you'll be creating eBooks using all of the applications we outline in chapter three) you should still assume that most readers will start out on page one and read some way into your book for a general introduction to the subject in hand before skipping to the sections most relevant to themselves.

The advice we gave in writing fiction therefore holds as true here as it does in what we can consider leisure writing. Grab your reader on page one, sentence one, and work as hard as you can to hold them with compelling pose throughout.

Images

'A picture is worth a thousand words.' Never has that been more true than it is in the world of digital publishing. Indeed, simple maths would suggest it's actually an understatement.

Despite the fact they're fundamentally different media, both text and images are built using tiny data sets called bits and bytes. Every byte is eight bits; every kilobyte is 1000 bytes, or about 200 words if your average word length is five characters. So, a 20GB raw image from your digital camera equates to 100,000 words.

A picture costs a thousand words, too...

As we'll explain later (see *Selling Your Book*), Amazon will will 'deliver' your book electronically for free if you opt for 35% royalties, but if you choose 70% it will charge you 10p (UK) or 15 cents (US and Canada) per megabyte to send it to your readers. The size of the book is calculated when you upload it, and the charge worked out pro-rata to the nearest kilobyte. So, a book that weighs in at 200KB would cost 2p or 3 cents to deliver, depending on territory, which would be deducted from your royalties.

Although words and numbers don't consume a great deal of either storage space or bandwidth when delivered, images are considerably more space-hungry, which is why comparatively few highly illustrated books have been converted for sale through the Kindle store. This is because each image must each be encoded and embedded within the book, and is the reason why the timeline graphics we'll be using in the book that we'll format and publish throughout this book have been kept very simple and rendered in just one colour.

It's worth thinking very carefully before including purely decorative images in your book – even as markers to appear at the end of a chapter or between sections. Often these can be replaced by regular characters which, however ornate they appear to be, would each only count as a single letter and so dramatically reduce the cost of delivering your book. Further, it is often better to simply leave a single blank line between sections within a chapter as readers are already familiar with this convention from its widespread use in printed books.

That doesn't mean you should shy away from using images, though. After all, there are times when including a picture, table or graph really would save you the trouble of writing a good 1000 words (or many more) as you struggle to explain a complex concept. Often the results will be more effective, too, helping your reader to grasp what it is you're trying to put across in a more effective manner.

If you don't believe us, try and envisage how you'd describe the contents of a Venn diagram in words alone without becoming hopelessly repetitive or confusing your audience.

Fortunately, with a little planning and forethought you can process your images so that they are better suited to use in a digital publication, and less expensive to ship to your audience.

Compression

The most effective measure you can employ is intelligent digital compression. Most photo-editing tools (such as the excellent Adobe Photoshop Elements) have a save-for-web option, which removes parts of the image that the human eye cannot detect. We're not talking about fine detail here, but variations in colour and texture that, if merged into their surroundings, wouldn't be missed.

The theory is that the human eye can detect changes in contrast far more effectively than it can changes in colour. So, an effective Jpeg compression tool would focus most of its attention on smoothing fine variations in colour across a wide area and avoid touching sharp edges such as lettering, lines and curves.

You can often compress a Jpeg image to around 60% of its original size without noticing any difference on a regular computer screen, and take simpler images down to around 30% of their original complexity before you start to seriously impact the results.

Spot the difference. The image on the left is saved at 100% quality and weighs in at 381KB. The image on the right is compressed to just 25% quality and consumes only 45KB without greatly affecting its appearance.

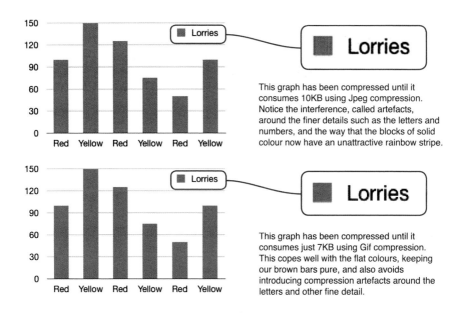

This graph has been compressed until it consumes 10KB using Jpeg compression. Notice the interference, called artefacts, around the finer details such as the letters and numbers, and the way that the blocks of solid colour now have an unattractive rainbow stripe.

This graph has been compressed until it consumes just 7KB using Gif compression. This copes well with the flat colours, keeping our brown bars pure, and also avoids introducing compression artefacts around the letters and other fine detail.

For every further 1% you can compress your image, you'll pay less. Or, to look at it from the opposite direction, you can include more images at the same cost, thus retaining a healthy profit margin while still producing a visually appealing product for your readers.

Colour

Not so long ago we would have recommended that you convert any images you intended to use in a book designed for reading back solely on an Amazon Kindle to greyscale. Like compression, this dramatically reduces the level of complexity in your image, and with it the size of the file.

However, with the arrival of the Kindle Fire that's no longer good advice. This 7in version of the company's best-selling reader is more accomplished than its siblings. Not only does it run a regular tablet operating system, meaning it's closer to a portable computer than a pure digital reading device, but it also boasts a backlit colour LCD screen.

It seems a shame not to take advantage of this where possible, and so although we wouldn't discourage you from including any greyscale images at all, it pays to treat your colour images with care and weigh up the various compression methods open to you.

Most web-save tools offer a choice of output formats, at the very least supplementing Jpeg with GIF (Graphics Interchange Format), which was initially introduced way back in 1987. This is particularly suited to presenting images with plenty of flat colour and sharp edges, such as business graphics and charts.

However, if used with care you can also use it for rendering less complex photos, as it is usually possible to specify the number of colours used to encode your image. The fewer colours you use, the smaller the resulting file.

Be careful how far you reduce the number of colours, as simplifying the image too much will introduce another problem: posterisation. When this occurs, what would once have been a smooth transition between differing tones becomes stepped. This is both distracting and undesirable – after all, have you ever seen stripes of different blue in the sky?

Fortunately you can reduce the strength of this undesirable effect by introducing dithering. This intersperses the light and dark tones within the image in a pattern that allows it to achieve a smoother result while not increasing the number of discrete tones used in the file.

Image size

Finally, check the size of your physical image and reduce it to fit within the likely resolution of the devices your audience will be using.

Amazon's 6in Kindles have screens that are 600 pixels across and 800 pixels tall. There's no point, therefore, in embedding 12-megapixel images, which are five times larger than those screens in each direction.

The iPad 2 display, meanwhile, has a slightly higher resolution of 768 x 1024, and the iPhone 4S, despite its 'retina' display in which the pixels are too small to be discerned by the naked human eye, tops out at just 640 x 960 pixels. In every instance, we've assumed that you're reading in portrait orientation.

Even if you choose not to apply any compression or colour reduction to your images, you should at least either crop or resize them to fit within those dimensions. Wherever possible, eBook covers should be sized to exactly fit the dimension of the screen for which they're designed so that they stretch from top to bottom and side to side, but if you're embedding images within your written content then pay particular attention to their widths, ensuring that they are narrower than the pages themselves. We would recommend keeping the final figure below 600 pixels wherever possible. If not, your readers' devices will shrink them to fit, throwing away a lot of unused data that you have needlessly paid to deliver to their ereader.

Embedding images

It's impossible to predict the full range of devices and applications your audience will use to access your book, so it's essential that you shoot for the lowest common denominator. That doesn't mean reverting to plain text – we've already ruled that out as unsuitable for profit-driven electronic publishing – but being conservative when it comes to formatting complex layouts that show off your content.

Apply only basic formatting to your images, remembering that they will be anchored within your text, rather than free to float on the screen. Placing an image immediately above or below a paragraph to which it relates means it can therefore stray onto the next page, or be left behind on the previous screen if it's unable to fit within the screen height of your reader's device.

Further, as they enlarge or reduce the text size, or change the font used to render it, the layout will constantly change, pushing images backwards and forwards across screen breaks.

If an image absolutely must appear beside a specific piece of text, therefore, reduce it to around 200 pixels in width, keeping its height in proportion, and embed it within the text, aligned to the left or to the right.

At 200 pixels it should be narrow enough for it to remain beside the text so long as your audience hasn't enlarged their font beyond a reasonable level, but you should still get into the habit of signposting particularly important graphics within your text. As a result, should they become detached from the content to which they relate, your audience still knows whether to look above, below, left or right.

Despite having one of the highest resolutions of any ereader, even the iPad can't display this 18-megapixel image without shrinking it down to fill the space at the centre of this frame. By shrinking the image yourself you'll produce a smaller file, which will cost you less to post.

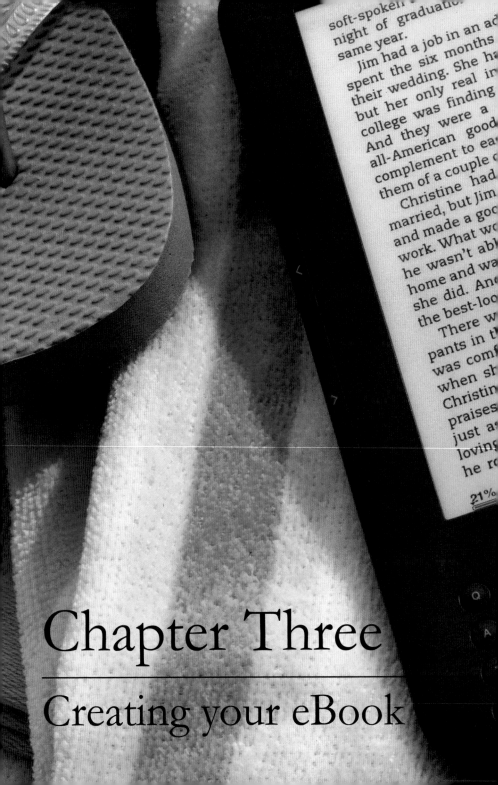

Chapter Three

Creating your eBook

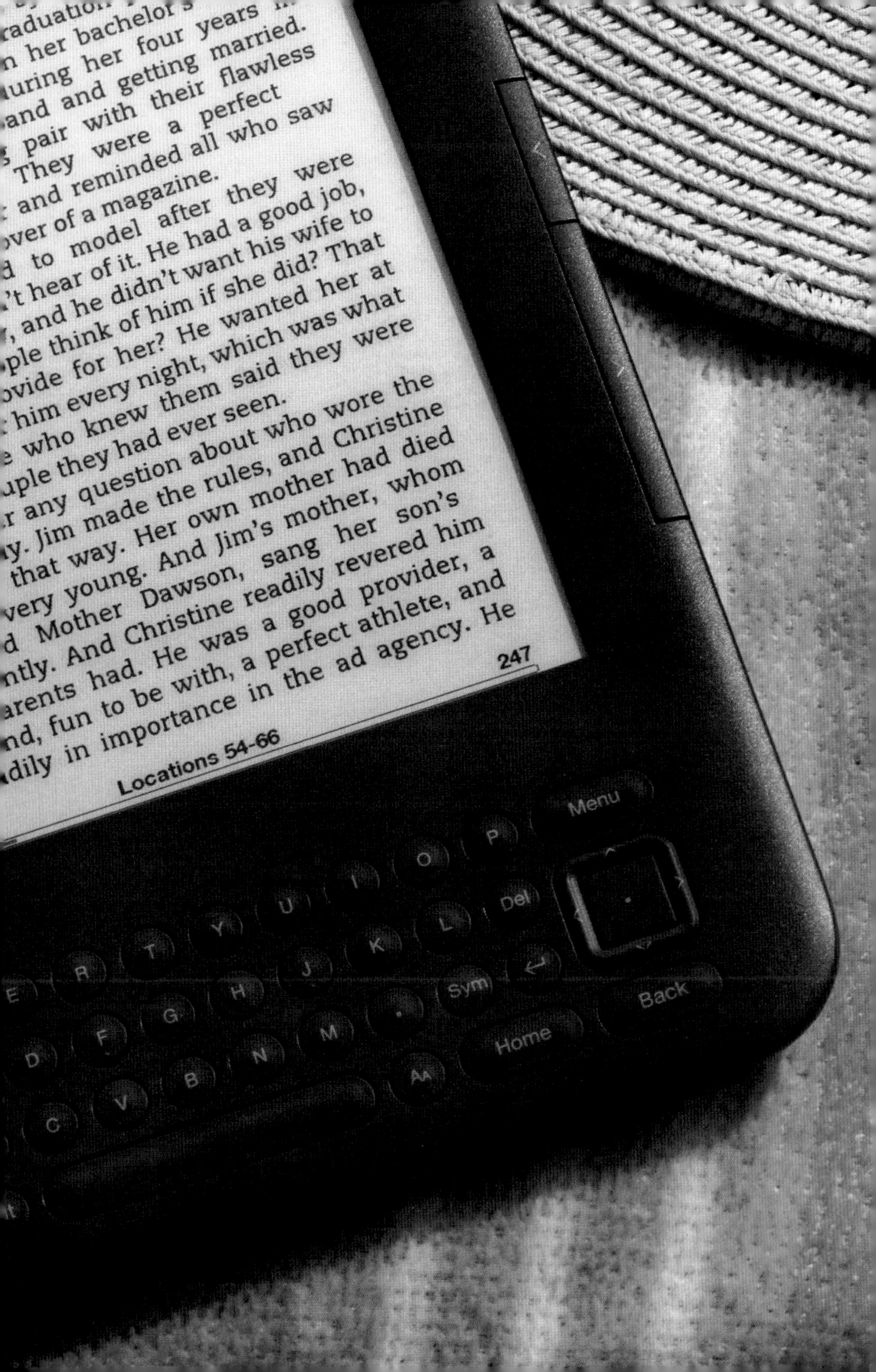
raduation
n her bachelor
uring her four years
and and getting married.
pair with their flawless
They were a perfect
and reminded all who saw
over of a magazine.
d to model after they were
't hear of it. He had a good job,
, and he didn't want his wife to
ple think of him if she did? That
vide for her? He wanted her at
him every night, which was what
who knew them said they were
uple they had ever seen.
r any question about who wore the
y. Jim made the rules, and Christine
that way. Her own mother had died
very young. And Jim's mother, whom
d Mother Dawson, sang her son's
ntly. And Christine readily revered him
arents had. He was a good provider, a
nd, fun to be with, a perfect athlete, and
dily in importance in the ad agency. He
247
Locations 54-66
Menu
Del
Sym
Back
Home

Formatting your eBook using Sigil

In the steps that follow we'll be using Sigil to format our book. Free to download from *code.google.com/p/sigil*, it's a cross-platform eBook editor that uses ePub as its native format. There are other platform-specific options, such as the excellent Scrivener on the Mac (at the time of writing Scrivener for Windows lacks eBook export options) but the following steps should work on both Macs and PCs.

Here we'll be working through the formatting of a genuine published Kindle book, The Sketchbook of John, Constable. If you'd like to follow along with a copy of the finished book in front of you, download a copy from Amazon UK at *http://amzn.to/gf7jFw* or from the US store at *http://amzn.to/u475sY*

Importing your raw copy

If your book is a plain text file then you have a head start, as you can open it directly inside Sigil and get working on it right away. However, if you wrote it using Word, you'll need to convert it first. From Word, pick File | Save As... and choose 'Web Page,

Sigil is a great option for first-time digital publishers, as it's free to download and uses ePub as its native file format. Here we have imported our raw book, having previously exported it from Microsoft Word.

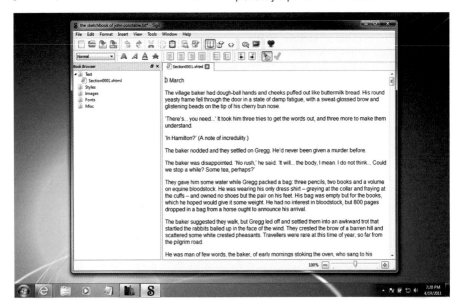

Filtered' as the format. Save the result in a location where you'll be able to find it easily, and open it in Sigil.

Just like web pages, ePub files are highly structured, with their contents described in underlying code and arranged in a particular order so that whatever ereader they are opened in will know exactly how to render their contents. Most ereaders, including the iBooks software that is free to download for use on the iPad, iPhone and iPod touch, use the ePub format. However, although Amazon hinted that it may also allow this format in the latest release of its devices, that never happened. We must, therefore, create Kindle-specific books if we want to sell them through its online store.

Our first job is to add the cover. Position your cursor at the very start of the text and press Ctrl-Shift-I (Command-Shift-I on the Mac) to open the image browser. Choose the picture you want to use and it will be added to the Images folder in the Sigil sidebar. At the moment it's nothing more than a floating asset in your raw ePub file and won't ever appear in the finished book until you tell the ereader how to use it. We do this using 'semantics', which as the name suggests is merely a signpost describing what the image is and how it should be used. We'll later go on to define different text types in exactly the same way.

Defining your cover

To mark out this image as the cover, then, right click its entry in the sidebar (command-click on the Mac) and choose Add Semantics | Cover Image.

Images that you want to embed within the text are imported in exactly the same way, but without being marked for use as the cover. In this book, The Sketchbook of John, Constable, we're using a graphic timeline at the start of

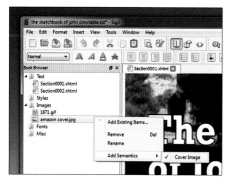

Once you have imported your cover image you need to define its use through the Add Semantics sub-menu. This image will be used in most cataloguing applications and on an ereader screen.

each chapter that would be impossible to render accurately using text. You can see what this looks like over the page. Although it looks large, the Kindle will automatically resize it to fit within the bounds of the screen when it appears in your finished book.

At this early stage, your book is a fairly unmanageable tract – just a long stretch of unformatted text – that needs to be split into chapters. Position your cursor at the very start of chapter one, immediately after the cover image, and press Ctrl-Return (Command-Return on the Mac) to insert a chapter break. Do the same at the start of chapter two. You will now have three files in the sidebar's Text folder with consecutive numbers. *Section0001.*

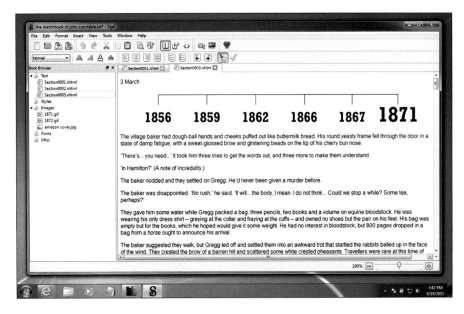

xhtml is your cover, *Section0002.xhtml* is chapter one and *Section0003.xhtml* is the rest of your book, which still needs to be further broken down. Continue working through the text, inserting a break before each chapter to create new files in the sidebar until you come to the end of the text.

Index your book with an active table of contents

If you want to include a table of contents in your book, use the style menu on the left of the toolbar as you create your chapters to mark each title as a Heading.

A table of contents is a mere formality in fiction books, and you can safely skip this step if you choose: few readers will want to skip straight to a particular section without having first read up to it. In this case, their ereader would save their position and present it the next time they switched it on or opened

Above, we have started work on splitting our book into chapters and also embedded the timeline graphic that will run across the top of each chapter. Our audience's ereaders will resize this to fit each device screen horizontally, while keeping the vertical measurement in proportion to avoid squashing the characters.

Although we have already split our book into chapters, they won't be indexed on the Contents screen unless we select them in Sigil's Table Of Contents Editor.

the book from the home screen. For a non-fiction book, however, a table of contents is far more important, as it helps your reader to identify specific sections that will be of interest and useful in research.

An accurate and comprehensive table of contents is often the factor by which print-published non-fiction either thrives or dies and there's no reason to assume that digital books should be considered in any other manner.

There are six heading styles to choose from, with Heading 1 uppermost in the hierarchy. Use them selectively, with Heading 1 applied to your chapter titles, Heading 2 to major sub-sections, Heading 3 to minor cross-headings, and so on. Press F7 to open the table of contents editor and uncheck any headings that you don't want to include in the table when you compile your book.

By now, your book is progressing well and you've done most of the grunt-work involved in defining sections already. You have split up your text into chapters and given each one a title so that it's easy to identify on the screen and can be navigated either by clicking the headings in the table of contents, or by using the Kindle's four-way rocker button, clicking left or right to jump backwards or forwards through the novel. You now need to think about how your book is going to be filed and sold online by adding all of the necessary author and title data that will identify it.

Adding index-ready metadata

Do this by pressing F8 to open the metadata editor and entering at the very least the title of your book and the author's name so that it can be accurately catalogued by online stores. To add further details such as the imprint, ISBN and rights, click More and use the Add Basic and Add Adv. buttons to add both common and more esoteric metadata. The more you add, the better your book will be catalogued.

When you've finished formatting your book, save it in Sigil's native ePub format. This is the format used by the majority of eBook readers, including iBooks on the iPad and iPhone, and for Kobo and other hardware readers, but not Kindle or Kindle apps, which use a modified version of Mobipocket. While the Kindle Direct Publishing process (see the chapter *Selling Your Book*) will handle the conversion, for the best and most predictable results you should perform the conversion yourself and test your book locally on your own Kindle wherever possible.

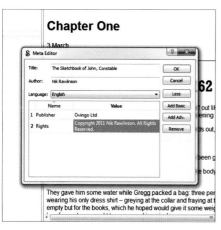

Metadata makes it easier for readers to find our book, as it will be more accurately filed in online stores.

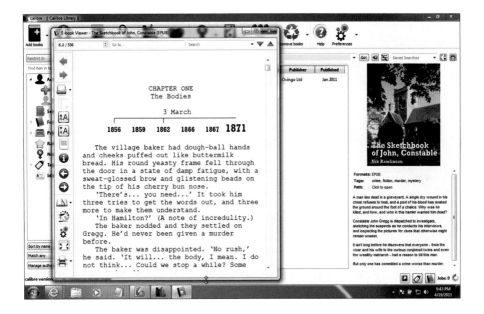

Importing your book to a Calibre library

We'll perform the conversion using Calibre, an open-source eBook library tool that's free to download from *calibre-ebook.com*. When you first install it you'll have to tell it where to file your library, but beyond that all management tasks, including conversions between different book formats, are conducted through the graphical user interface.

Check that your book has accurately imported into your Calibre library by double-clicking its entry in the list of titles. The text is unlikely to match your original font choice as each ereader applies its own settings, but you should be able to click through each of your pages using the purple arrow buttons in the sidebar.

You can add whole books or references to your Calibre library in a number of ways, from the simple step of entering an ISBN (see the chapter *Selling your eBook*) for which it will retrieve the cover art and metadata, to importing a complete book file for reading and manipulation. We need the latter, so click Add Books and navigate to your formatted epub document. Select the book and click OK. Calibre copies the book to its library and uses the metadata you entered in Sigil to catalogue it.

To check that it has accurately imported your book, double-click its cover in the library to preview the contents. You should be able to click to the start of each chapter in the table of contents, and click forwards and back through the pages using the purple arrows. If it works as you expect, you're ready to convert it to Kindle's native format.

Converting your book for Kindle use

Calibre can convert your eBook between a wide variety of formats, and has a specific setting for Kindle. However, as we can't be sure that all members of our potential audience will have a Kindle, we instead choose Generic e-ink as the output format when processing our existing ePub document.

Click Convert Books, and select Mobi as the output format from the pull-down menu at the top right of the conversion panel. The input format should already be set to ePub, our book's current format, as it will have been detected from the input file type.

Click Page Setup and work your way through the sections in the left-hand column. Most of them can be left at their default settings, but you should make sure you check that Generic e-ink is selected as the output profile. e-ink is the screen technology used by most ereaders that don't double up as tablet computers, and underpins every Amazon Kindle apart from the Kindle Fire, which uses a 7in backlit LCD.

There is a specific Kindle option elsewhere in the Output profile box, but as you can't be sure that all of your readers will be accessing the book on a Kindle it's best to avoid this option at this point.

When you have finished working through the various sections, click OK to perform the conversion. From here on everything is automated. The progress

Perform a final check of your converted book by connecting your Kindle using the bundled USB cable and transferring the file by dragging it across or using Calibre's Send to Device option.

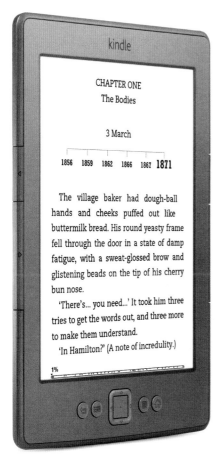

spinner at the bottom of the library window will show you it's working, but when it stops it won't be immediately obvious where it's put the completed document. To find it, select the book in the library and click the link beside Path in the book details pane.

Upload your file to a Kindle... and test, test, test

Connect your Kindle to a free USB port and either drag the Mobipocket-formatted book to its Documents folder, or use the 'Send to device' button on the Calibre toolbar to upload it. You can then eject your Kindle in the usual way before disconnecting.

Your new book will appear at the top of the Kindle home screen. Open it to check that it looks like you expected and that you're happy for it to be published on Amazon in this form. Check in particular that the table of contents is in tact (press Menu | Go to... | table of contents) and that clicking the links there takes you to the relevant points in the book. Further, check that your chapter markers are in place. These are the notches cut into the progress bar at the foot of the reading display. Using the left- and right-hand edges of the four-way controller skips you backwards and forwards a chapter at a time, rather than moving page by page.

If it all works as you expected, you're ready to take the final step and publish your book on Amazon. We cover the upload, pricing and selling process in detail, starting with the chapter *Selling Your eBook*.

Now check the ePub version of your document and select an online store or stores through which to sell it, choosing the same price as you did for your Kindle edition.

Formatting your eBook using Scrivener

Scrivener started life as a Mac-only writing tool that has steadily built itself a well deserved, loyal following among full-time wordsmiths. Its unique feature is the ability to split long work projects into individual documents, which can be rearranged within the overall project file as the structure of your overall document changes.

This is particularly attractive to anyone writing digital books for sale as ePub or Kindle files, as the individual files can also be used as the break between chapters in a compiled book, allowing you to produce fully indexed, properly threaded digital books without manually splitting the work file, as we did when formatting our novel using Sigil.

Scrivener has since appeared on Windows and is available in beta form for Linux users, but these platforms currently don't enjoy the eBook

Scrivener lets you organise each separate part of your book into folders for chapters and files for scenes. Overall containing folders also help you define more general sections within the book.

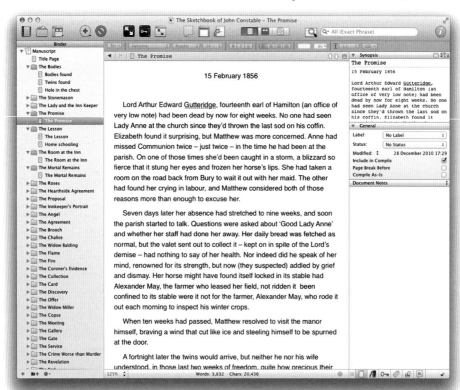

publishing tools available to Mac users. What follows, then, will be of interest only to Mac users running version 2 or later of Scrivener (unless Scrivener releases an update for PC users). You can download a free trial for each platform from *literatureandlatte.com*.

Structure your book

Launch Scrivener and start a new work file. The application comes bundled with document types for various different types of creative work, including both fiction and non-fiction. The fiction documents are a great place to start if you're writing for print publication and want to use a format that meets agents' and publishers' requirements. You'll be publishing your own book, though, so skip these on this occasion and choose the Blank document type. Click Choose... and give your document a name.

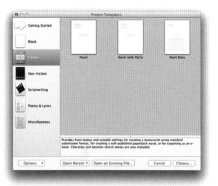

Scrivener comes bundled with a generous range of document types to get you started.

Your first task is to decide on a structure. You can tailor this as you go through, but start by creating a folder for each of your chapters using the keyboard shortcut command-alt-N. Give each one a name, or a chapter number ('Chapter 1', 'Chapter 2' etc). When you come to compile your book you can opt to use these as automatically generated chapter titles and content list entries.

We have chosen to give each of our chapters a descriptive name rather than a number-based title so that should we choose to reorganise them later in our project we won't have to rename them to keep them in numerical order.

Now create a new file within each folder for each scene in your story (command-N). Clearly if you haven't planned your story or work of non-fiction in advance you won't be able to do this at this stage, so if you don't want to sit down and work out your flow immediately, simply create your first document in your first folder and start writing.

Reorganising your book

We'll start on the task of writing the book in a moment, but before we do, we need to touch on Scrivener's organisational tools.

Once you have defined the structure of your book using files and folders, you can use its document structuring tools to re-work the flow of your book and get a better overview of the way in which your document proceeds.

Sometimes it only becomes clear once you're well into a project how your

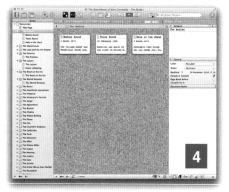

Scrivener document views. (1) Text-editing view, with the left-channel binder showing each chapter folder and scene document. (2) Outliner view, showing a summary of each scene in the book. (3) Corkboard view, allowing you to drag complete chapters into a new order. (4) Another corkboard view, this time showing just the scenes within chapter 1, allowing them to be reorganised without affecting the overall chapter flow.

story needs to be told, or your non-fiction thesis is best explained. On these occasions you'll want to change the order of your work on the fly, either by dragging individual scene files out of their existing chapters and into new ones, or by moving whole chapters, including all of their contents.

The default text-editing view (1, above) gives you the best of both worlds, allowing you to re-organise your document structure in the binder sidebar while viewing each complete document in the main editing window (selecting a chapter folder organises each of the scenes in a single view, with horizontal dividers between them). The outliner (2) compresses each scene into a summary within the chapter folder, that can be dragged within the structure. Additional columns let you set tags to define draft stages and set target word or character counts. The corkboard view, meanwhile, is the most compact, presenting your work on index cards that can be dragged in the same way you might scatter ideas on a desk, or arrange them in a cogent flow that comes to form the basis of your book.

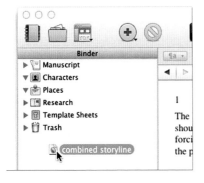

Writing your book

With your basic structure in place you can start work on your content. By far the easiest way to work is to type directly into your book file within Scrivener, but if you have already written your book in another application, import the document by dragging it into the sidebar (*left*), and then copy and paste the sections into your scene documents.

Don't spend too much time worrying about the choice of font or its size as it is unlikely that what you set here will be accurately reflected in your audience's ereaders, since they each sport a different range of built-in fonts. However, do think about relative formatting – that is, the size of characters in relation to each other. Use the built-in paragraph styles, accessed through the toolbar's pilcrow (¶) button, which gives you access to headings, sub-headings, titles and body text. Further, careful use of bold, italic and underline should be carried across to your audience's ereaders once you have exported the file.

Working with covers and images

The book we are formatting here, *The Sketchbook of John, Constable*, calls for an opening graphic at the start of each chapter, which explains where the action takes place within a storyline spanning 15 years. As explained in the previous section – Sigil – this has been rendered in a single colour to reduce the amount of storage space it consumes and thus minimise the download costs incurred by each sale.

This can be simply dragged in (*below*) from the OS X Finder and dropped in

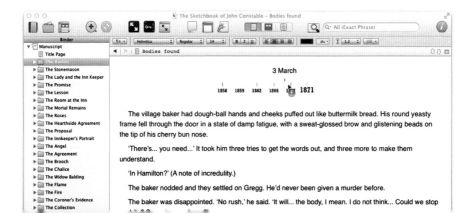

position on the page. We have chosen to centre this in our document – a simple formatting convention that will be accurately carried over into your compiled eBook. You can resize your images by double-clicking them and using the sliders to adjust the vertical and horizontal measurements, but we're leaving ours as it is so that the ereaders used to render it can resize it to fit their screen widths.

Finally, you need to add a cover. This isn't embedded within any of your documents the way it is in Sigil, but dropped in the sidebar the same way as your source files and referenced during the compilation process.

Compiling your book

Scrivener can handle compiling your book into both Kindle and ePub formats, but requires that you manually install and locate Amazon's KindleGen driver before it can handle Kindle conversions. Download this from *amazon.com/ kindlepublishing*, save it on your Mac and locate it by selecting *Kindle eBook (.mobi)* from the *Compile For:* menu at the bottom of the pull-down dialogue and clicking the *Change...* button to locate the file (*right*). You only need do this once and it'll be set for all future compilations.

Click 'Contents' in the dialogue sidebar and select the sections you want to include. Check both the chapter folders and the scenes that they contain before moving on to the 'Separators' dialogue, which controls what happens between each folder and file. Set the *'Text'* and *'Folder and text'* separators to *'Empty line'*, and both the *'Folder'* and *'Text and folder'* separators to *'Section break'* (*right*). This will split your compiled document according to your defined chapters and use these breaks in the compilation of your contents section. On the Kindle it will also insert notches on the progress bar, which your readers can use with the four-way controller to skip directly to your chapter openings.

Click *Cover* and use the *Cover image* drop-down menu to select the cover file you dragged into your sidebar. A preview of the selected image will appear in the box below, so you can check you have selected the right one if you have

Above: Before compiling for Kindle you'll need to download the KindleGen add-on and tell Scrivener where to find it.

Below: Breaking your compiled eBook into chapters is a simple matter of telling Scrivener to insert section breaks before each defined folder within your work file.

When he tired of making scant progress, he looked again at the Balding house, but that was barely more helpful.

The twins' portrait was still too good to be of any great use. A medical journal might like to have bought it, or maybe a pier-end circus show, for the likeness could barely be faulted, and that made it fairly well useless. It showed well enough what

60%

Set Scrivener to put a section break before each folder. When compiling your book it will insert chapter markers throughout your file for easy navigation using the Kindle's four-way controller.

The more metadata you add, the more accurately your book will be filed. Although a copyright notice will do little to deter less ethical users from pirating your work, it's also worth asserting your rights here.

dragged different versions into the sidebar to cater for alternative markets or the different size requirements of a selection of targeted ereaders.

Skip to the *Layout* section and make sure *'Generate HTML table of contents'* is checked if you want one of these to appear at the start of your document.

Finally, click the *Meta-Data* section and enter your identifying data. Make sure that at the very least you add your name and the title of your book to ensure it's accurately filed by the online stores through which you choose to sell it, and on your readers' devices.

We would recommend, however, that you go further than this, by asserting your rights (*left*) and writing a short description, which can be the same as the synopsis you submit to Amazon and other online stores. If you are writing a non-fiction book, you should also get into the habit of tagging it with comma-separated keywords in the *Subject* box, as this may help boost your book's search performance within online stores.

When you've finished working your way through this dialogue, click *Compile* and choose both a file name and location in which to save it.

Although you have saved your first eBook, the text is preserved in its original state within your Scrivener work file, which means you can make another book – either ePub or Mobipocket – using whichever format you passed over for the first version by again selecting it from the *Compile For:* drop-down.

Formatting your eBook using InDesign

Exporting your book directly from a desktop publishing application such as InDesign or QuarkXPress can lead to problems if not handled with care. Each of these applications is tailored towards producing complex page layouts in which elements are anchored precisely on the page, allowing you to predict with great certainty where an image will appear and how the text will run around it.

That's not the case with electronic books, in which the text flows according to the reader's current settings, orientation, font face, text size and screen dimensions. A certain degree of simplification therefore has to take place.

Fortunately Amazon has simplified the task of producing electronic books for Kindle with the introduction of the Kindle Plugin for InDesign CS4, CS5 and CS5.5, thus saving legacy users from upgrading to the latest edition. If you also want to produce ePub versions of your book you then have two options: either to upgrade to InDesign CS 5.5, which introduces dedicated ePub publishing tools, or use Calibre to perform a conversion (*see p36*).

The Kindle Plugin for InDesign produces books compliant with KF8 format, which is Amazon's largely HTML-based replacement for Mobipocket. Currently only Kindle Fire supports all of the features of KF8, including table formatting and drop shadows, but books produced using this plug-in degrade gracefully to also render accurately on a regular e-ink-based Kindle.

Install the plugin

The Kindle plugin is a free download for both Mac and Windows users from *amazon.com/kindlepublishing*. Once installed, launch InDesign and you'll see that it has added a new item to the File menu: *Export for Kindle...*

This will bundle together your text and images, split your book into chapters, build a table of contents and package the project in a Kindle-compatible format.

Formatting your book

If you're writing your book from scratch for purely digital distribution, we'd recommend sticking with Scrivener or Sigil; if you're working in InDesign it's either because you want to repurpose an existing product, or you need to lay out a dual-purpose print and digital book for simultaneous distribution. You therefore need to think carefully about the styles you use and, in particular, their names.

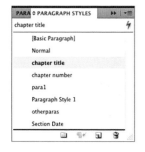

If you're starting from scratch, then define at the very least a plain body paragraph style and a title style, which in our example we've called chapter title (*left*). If this doesn't make any sense in your workflow, you can choose an alternative – just so long as you can later use it in the creation of your table of contents.

In this particular case we were working on the conversion of an existing book (again, we're using *The Sketchbook of John, Constable*), which introduces a number of complications that must be overcome. Originally it was formatted such that a chapter number headed each section break, followed by the chapter title on the next line. However, because we wanted our table of contents to use the chapter names to link to the start of each section, rather than the less meaningful number, we couldn't define the number as a chapter marker. Instead we used the chapter names as the markers so that they would be correctly copied across to the table of contents. As each chapter always began on a new page this wasn't a problem, as we could still guarantee that the number and name would appear on the same page when printed. However, this meant that technically the chapter started one line *after* the chapter number, and so the plugin correctly appended that number to the end of the previous chapter. That's not what our readers would expect at all.

We therefore reformatted our document, moving the chapter number to the start of the line containing the chapter name and styling the complete line using the '*chapter title*' paragraph style.

As we were working on the conversion of an existing book, our complex formatting caused some problems, with chapter titles appearing after chapter numbers, and the timeline breaking during conversion.

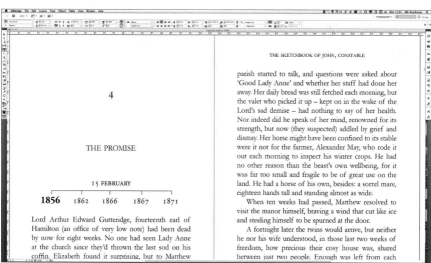

We had originally rendered the timeline that appeared at the start of each chapter as a line of spaced text with the current year in a larger typeface, and used pen strokes to define the structure (*see previous page*). However, this doesn't transfer accurately to KF8 format, which strips out the strokes and bunched the timeline dates – which had previously been overlaid in a grouped frame – on the left of the line. We had to decide on an alternative solution. The simplest – which we chose – was to put the year immediately at the end of the date line, although we could have used the same flat graphic as we did in the Sigil and Scrivener formatting projects.

Despite this work-around, the plugin can convert most common formatting conventions, including regular alignment (away from/towards spine respectively align to the right and left following conversion) and paragraph spacing, with all Kindles respecting left and right indents, first line indent and space both above and below paragraphs. This latter point is important since multiple line breaks will be merged into one. If you want to insert a considerable gap between running sections within your book you'll need to format them as space below the preceding paragraph.

Defining your table of contents

Although we have used the paragraph style 'chapter title' to mark out the start of each chapter, this convention is for our own benefit alone, and means nothing to the conversion plugin. To build a functioning table of contents, you therefore need to either place a table within your document, if you want to define precisely the place within the flow of the book where it will appear in your compiled eBook, or simply define a style if you are happy for the plugin to position it, as default, at the start of the book.

If you want to control where it appears, then create a page or spread, depending on its size, wherever in your publication you want to locate the table and pick *Layout | Table of Contents...* Use the dialogue to define which heading styles should be included in the table, including at the very least your *chapter title* style and any sub-styles you have defined throughout your document. Don't worry at this stage about styling it: the plugin will remove your defined styles when compiling your book, along with the page numbers themselves, which are irrelevant in a dynamically-set document. Make a note of the 'TOC Style' (in this case, '*[Default]*') and then click OK. Click on your spread where you'd like to

Use InDesign's integrated Table of Contents editor to build your own linked index for non-fiction books.

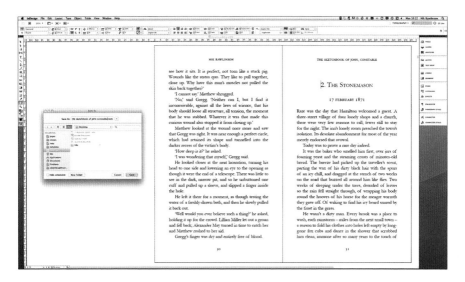

When you're ready to convert your book, select a location and give it a name, retaining the .mobi extension required by Kindle devices.

position your table of contents and it will create its own text frame and flow in the copy.

If you prefer not to place a table of contents in your book, then instead select *Layout | Table of Contents styles...* This calls up the same dialogue as we used to originally define our table of contents (*left*), but doesn't expect you to place it at the end of the process.

Compiling your eBook

You're now ready to perform the conversion. Select *File | Export for Kindle...*, set a location and give your book a name, leaving the .mobi extension in place to mark it out as a Mobipocket-formatted book (*above*). This calls up the export dialogue, which controls the way in which your book is compiled. The most important pages are the first and third – General and Metadata.

General

This dialogue defines the look and feel of your eBook. Check the box to include InDesign's table of contents (TOC) entries and make sure the *TOC Style* you noted earlier appears in the *TOC Style* box so that your defined entries are carried across. Now attach a cover by clicking the button to the right of the Cover Image box, navigating to the cover on your hard drive and selecting it. You won't get a preview as you do with Scrivener, but you will see its location in the Cover Image box, so make sure you have selected the right file before progressing any further.

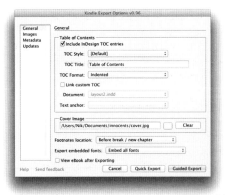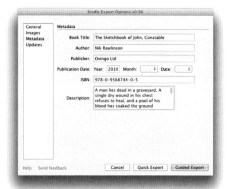

Above: the General (left) and Metadata (right) export dialogues in Amazon's Kindle Plugin for InDesign give you control over the conversion process that turns the pages you designed for print into an electronic book.

Finally on this screen, decide whether you want to embed the fonts you have used in the layout within your eBook file. If you do, then KF8-compatible devices (which at the moment includes only the Kindle Fire) will use the same fonts as you have used in your original layout. However, this is not without its disadvantages. Most importantly, embedding fonts will increase the size of your download, which will therefore reduce your profit per sale for – considering the size of the potential audience at the moment – very little benefit.

Further, you should only choose to embed fonts for which you have distribution rights. That means not using commercial fonts unless your licence specifically permits redistribution through embedding.

If you have any doubts at all, then, change the *Export embedded fonts* option to *Don't embed any fonts* and allow your audience's ereaders to use their default font settings.

Metadata

The metadata dialogue is where you specify the data that describes your book. It's attached to the digital file, so should be used to detail the title, your name, your publishing company (if applicable) and add a short description. Although you'll repeat a lot of this when you upload your book to Amazon, the more you add here, the better, as it will always be available for use in the future.

Amazon has a number of guidelines that should be followed to ensure the metadata is properly indexable. If you are publishing both an eBook and a printed version of your work, then the book title used on the eBook should, wherever possible, match that on the printed book. Clearly, if you're running a digital-only workflow, this won't apply to you.

Author names should follow the convention surname, suffix, given name, initial. So, Nik Rawlinson, for whom there is no suffix, would be *Rawlinson, Nik J,* while multiple authors should have their names separated by a semicolon, following the same convention: *Rawlinson, Nik J; Aleksandr Jnr., Lukas P*

Make sure you specify at least a year in the date box, or the other information you enter will be ignored. Plus, when you're typing the description box, use control and enter to add a line break to your copy.

The *Updates* pane controls only how (and if) your plugin updates itself, while the *Images* pane lets you tailor the way in which your embedded graphics are optimised for delivery. If you have already optimised your graphics externally using regular editing tools such as Photoshop, Paint Shop Pro or Gimp then you can leave this set to default. Kindle Plugin can handle any Gif, Bmp, Jpeg and Png graphics (it converts them to Jpeg or Gif) and will reduce the file size of any larger than 127KB without changing their physical on-page dimensions (although they will be dynamically resized by the ereader to fit on its screen).

If you have disabled the option to embed fonts in your eBook you can now click *Quick Export* to complete the process and compile the publication; otherwise, click *Guided Export* and select the fonts you want to include, remembering that the fewer you embed, the smaller your eventual file.

Publishing native ePub files using InDesign CS 5.5

Although you can convert your Kindle files to ePub format, Adobe has also integrated ePub compilation tools – although no Kindle tools – in InDesign CS 5.5 and above. These make use of the new Articles pane to define the structure and flow of an exported ePub document.

The workflow is extremely simple: once you have laid out your document you simply drag your assets from the page – including whole text frames, complete with their flowed content – onto the panel where they are listed in order. Dragging them within the pane lets you then move them within the final exported document.

InDesign CS 5.5 and later includes an Articles panel, which allows you to define which content should appear in your compiled ePub book and the order in which it flows.

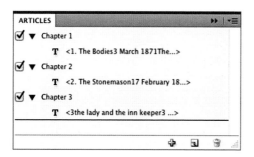

The process is a little more involved than Amazon's largely automated workflow, but the results are more flexible and easy to mould to your exact requirements.

Further, as the content appearing in the Articles pane is merely a tagged, ordered copy of the text and graphics on your page, making last minute changes to the laid-out original means they will also be reflected in any subsequently compiled eBook.

Formatting your eBook using QuarkXPress

Like InDesign, QuarkXPress has long played a leading role in the production of complex laid-out documents. For many years it was the default choice for magazine and newspaper publishers as the only realistic option for reliably producing heavyweight documents encompassing large quantities of text and images.

That changed when Adobe entered the market with InDesign and started to steal Quark's customers, but in recent years, thanks to a series of ever-improving, more powerful and more flexible releases, Quark has proved that it remains a key player in the field of professional publishing, and in no realm less than digital production.

QuarkXPress 9.2 supports ePub 3.0 publishing, a standard which includes support for embedded video and audio. The ePub format is compatible with iPad, Kobo, Nook, Sony Reader and the majority of other third-party devices, but not natively compatible with the Kindle, which will require conversion either manually (as we would recommend, using Calibre or equivalent) or during the upload and approval process by Amazon.

Here we'll walk through the process of reformatting existing copy as eBook content using the integrated *Reflow* view. We'll be using a Mac, but as QuarkXPress is a cross-platform product you can achieve the same results on a PC running Windows.

Setting up your document

We're going to create our book from scratch, flowing in copy that we have already written elsewhere in a third-party word processing tool. The first step, then, is to define a new project from the File menu, and select *ePUB* as the Layout Type (*right*).

Although we're creating a purely digital product that will never be printed we still need to provide a guideline size that matches the dimensions of its virtual cover. We have no way of knowing exactly what ereading device our audience will be using, so we can't target their screen sizes precisely, and in this case we've picked 1024 x 768 pixels, portrait orientation. This matches the resolution of the current-generation iPad 2. We want our

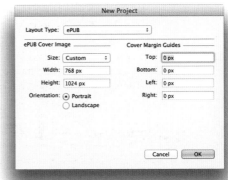

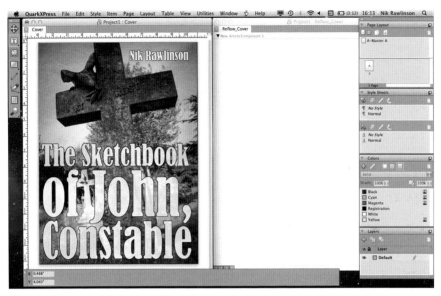

When creating a new ePub document, QuarkXPress creates two document windows – one for your cover, on the left, and one for the content of your book, on the right. The cover document size is defined during the set-up process, so specify a size that matches your original artwork.

cover to stretch from top to bottom of the screen, and side to side, so we've also left the cover margin guides set to 0px.

Adding a cover

Now that we've defined the document size, it's time to add a cover. This needs to match the dimensions defined when creating the document if you don't want to stretch it to fit. Click in the Cover window and pick *File | Import* and navigate to the cover graphic on your hard drive to drop it on the page.

Importing your content

That completes the admin tasks involved in setting up your document. From here on in you'll start working with your live text.

Because we chose to create an ePub document from scratch, QuarkXPress has set us up with just one reflow article, which currently comprises the blank document *Reflow_Cover*, to the right of the *Cover* window. This is where we will paste all of our content. There is no option to create multiple windows and gather together a collection of documents as they would be ignored in the compilation process. Further, the range of formatting options has been kept

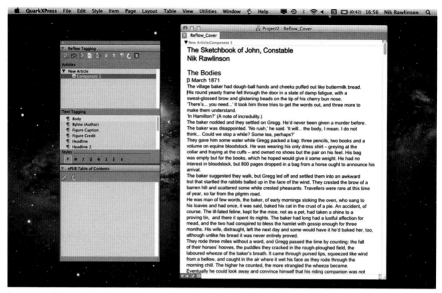

It isn't possible to create further document windows as the content of your book is flowed in as a single stream of formatted text. This is broken up during the compilation process at points defined using styles and Articles during the layout process.

deliberately narrow to ensure that any applied styles will transfer correctly to the widest possible range of ereading devices.

At the moment your document will have only one article in place, called *New Article*, containing one component. You can see it listed in the *Reflow Tagging* window. Components are the various media elements that make up each article, comprising text, graphics, audio and video – the latter two only used in enhanced ePub 3.0 documents.

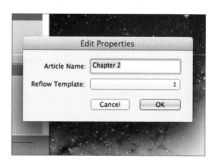

Copy the first chapter of your book from whichever text editor you have used to write it, and paste it into the *Reflow_Cover* window.

You now need to create a new article to hold chapter two. Click the *New Article* button on the *Reflow Tagging* palette – the first button – followed immediately by *Edit Properties* – the third button – to change its name to something that makes more sense. In the example, *above*, we've called ours Chapter 2. QuarkXPress inserts a break in your document, which will be used as a chapter break when you compile your eBook and open it in an ePub-compatible ereader device.

Add a new *Text Component* (second button) and select it in the *Reflow Tagging* palette, before pasting in the second chapter of your book into the new Component within the *Reflow_Cover* window.

QuarkXPress marks the breaks in your document with a dotted line and the name of each component (*see below*), which is mirrored in the *Reflow Tagging* palette. It takes a little more effort, but it's well worth renaming each of these as you create them so that you can rearrange them within the palette to change the running order of your document.

By default, all of your text will have the *Body* style applied to it at this stage. This is left aligned, using a standard font, which will be swapped out by your audience's devices' default typeface. You can add basic formatting to these default styles, such as bold, italic, underline, strikethrough, super- and sub-script to help clarify the meaning and flow of your content. Use these to selectively apply emphasis to your text before moving on to using the text tags to start building your table of contents.

Applying text tags to your content

Text tags are the pre-defined styles – analogous to paragraph styles in regular print-based layout – used to pick out particular text types in your document. They are also used to filter which parts

Each element of your eBook is contained within its own Article (here, called *Chapter 2*), as a distinct component. Components can consist of text, graphics and embedded audio or video.

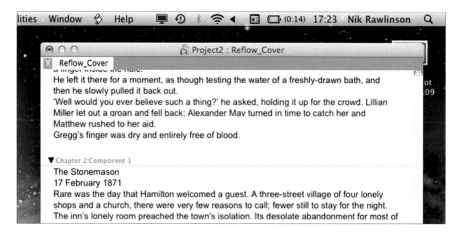

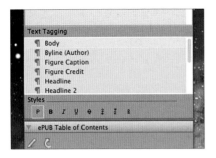

The contents of the Text Tagging pane are used to define the different types of text that make up your document, which is more important than applying visual styles to each one.

of the document should be hyperlinked in your table of contents.

Position your cursor at the start of your first chapter and, if you don't already have one, add a chapter title, then click *Section / Chapter Name* in the Text Tagging panel.

This enlarges the text and centres it, making it easier to pick out as a heading, but its real purpose is to define the role of that particular element so that we can go on to re-use it later on during the compilation process.

Work your way through the rest of your book, applying headings at the start of each chapter and using the *Headline* and *Headline 2* styles to mark out subheadings embedded within the text and make it easier to navigate. Non-fiction authors should include these within their table of contents; fiction writers will be able to stick with the *Section / Chapter Name* style.

Building your table of contents

The table of contents allows your readers to skip straight to particular sections of your book in the same way that an index page on a website lets visitors click on links to switch to new pages.

You can use as many tags as you want within your table of contents, but for the moment we're going to stick to the two defined above for chapter openings

The Table of Contents palette will update itself automatically as you add headings and chapter names to your document.

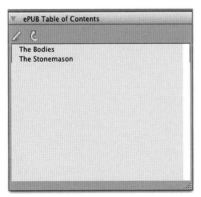

and headlines. By default these are already selected within the Table of Contents builder, so as you apply the tags within your document you'll see each heading appear in the *ePUB Table of Contents* palette (*left*). If they don't, click the green curled arrow to update the table manually.

If you are writing a technical document, you'll need to add other copy types, such as pull quotes, figures and both ordered and unordered lists to your table of contents so that your readers can skip to them directly without reading through the surrounding text.

Do this by clicking the pencil icon to open the Reflow Table of Contents Editor (*see over*). Use the arrows to move element types into and out of the table by shifting them from the

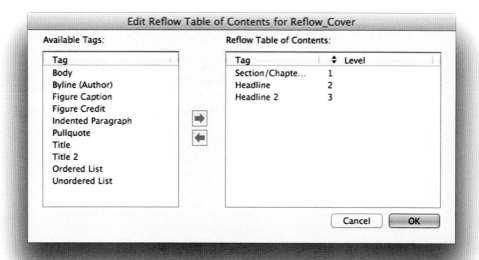

well of available tags into the Reflow Table of Contents.

The Reflow Table of Contents editor lets you define which defined document elements should be linked in the table of contents and their prominence in the list.

It's important to strike a balance between building a comprehensive table of contents and keeping from overwhelming your reader here. Don't include your secondary headlines if they are merely pointers used to break the flow of long tracts of text as they will make the table of contents difficult to navigate and impossible to skim-read.

Once you have included all of the document elements you need to show in your table, you'll have to define a clear hierarchy. This is detailed in the Level column, where Level 1 is the most important element, Level 2 the second most important and so on. Click on each element in turn, and then click the Level heading at the top of the columns to assign its score (*right*).

When you compile your book those elements on Level 1 will be aligned flush with the left edge of the digital page, while Levels 2, 3 and so on will be increasingly indented.

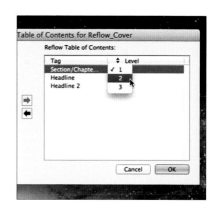

Adding your eBook metadata

The last job to complete before compiling the book is to add the metadata that will both brand your book and make it easier to catalogue.

Click *Layout | eBook Metadata...* to open the metadata editor (*left*). Add, at the very least, the title of your book and your author name. If you have set up your own publishing imprint (*see p94*) and received a batch of ISBN numbers, assign one to your book, remembering to inform your issuing agency, and detail it here. You can use the same details in the *Description* field as you will on your store listing.

This is the last stage in building the content of your book; you're now ready to compile it into an ePub for submission to your outlets of choice.

Compiling your ePub document

Pick *File | Export | Layout as ePUB* and give your document a name. By default QuarkXPress will set the ePub style to *Captured Settings*, which uses the settings detected in your source document. If this causes any problems in your testing phase then change it to *Default ePUB Output Style* and compile for a second time before retesting.

Click *Options...* to check the detected settings and tweak the image export settings. Keep the image resolution at 72ppi to avoid overloading your document with bloated images that will increase the cost of each download, thus reducing your profits, and choose an export format and image quality. QuarkXPress offers a choice of PNG and Jpeg, neither of which should cause any problems for the current range of ereaders on sale.

Before submitting your compiled document to an online store, test it on an ereader device and use EpubCheck to ensure it correctly validates (see p74).

Click the Table of Contents entry and check that the exporter is set to build this *From ePUB TOC Palette*, then OK out of the dialogue and save your file.

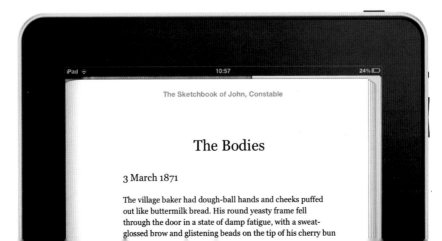

Publishing your eBook using iBooks Author

When Apple announced iBooks Author, alongside iBooks 2, the update to its ereading software for the iPad, iPhone and iPod touch, it claimed it would revolutionise textbook publishing. Clearly it had done its homework. At launch, Apple had already convinced many professionals – teachers and publishers alike – that its vision was a viable one, as the glossy promotional video on its website contained plenty of impressive endorsements.

The software itself is free, and can be downloaded from the OS X App Store. That means it won't run on a PC, nor on an older Mac with a PowerPC processor. This is a clever move on Apple's part, as iBooks Author not only heightens the iPad's appeal to those developing academic eBooks, but also helps it to sell more Macs into the professional publishing field.

iBooks Author follows very similar lines to Apple's office suite, iWork, with templates to get you started (*right*), and a simple drag-and-drop workflow once you start working on your book. This means you don't need to spend hours working out how your book should flow before you start putting in your content, and allows even non-technical, non-trained designers to work on the layout of their own book in the knowledge that they'll produce an impressive set of results.

However, it's not without its limitations. Because you are always working with a template it's easy to produce books that look very similar to others built using iBooks Author. As we'll show you in this section, though, each is incredibly flexible, allowing you to change their layouts, resize their placeholder images and reformat their sample text until you have created something that more accurately reflects the subject about which you're writing.

iBooks Author documents don't follow regular ePub conventions. Apple has, instead, mixed existing ePub standards, some unratified elements and its own extensions to produce very impressive results. Again, though, this introduces one very serious limitation: the number of platforms on which you can publish. iBooks Author books can only be read on an iPad. They are designed specifically for its 9.7in screen, and because of the extensions used in their underlying code you won't be able to port them to a third-party ereading device. Your only choices are therefore to export your pages as PDF documents from within the application, or start the work all over again – from scratch – in one of the other applications outlined here to produce an open ePub version.

The final limitation comes in what you can do with your finished product. If you want to give it away – for free – then you needn't worry: you can do this whenever and wherever you want. However, the terms of the End User License Agreement (EULA) clearly state that if you want to make money from your work then separate rules apply:

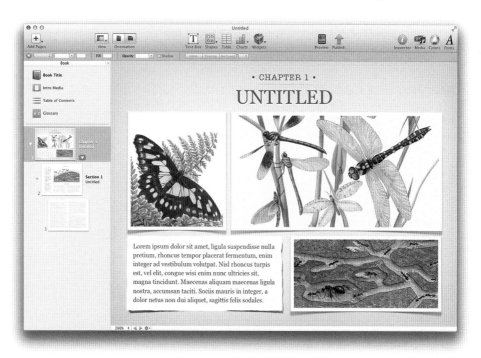

> ❝ ... if the work is provided for free (at no charge), you may distribute it by any means; if the work is provided for a fee (including as part of any subscription-based product or service) and includes files in the .ibooks format generated using iBooks Author, the work may only be distributed through Apple, and such distribution will be subject to a separate written agreement with Apple (or an Apple affiliate or subsidiary); provided, however, that this restriction will not apply to the content of the work when distributed in a form that does not include files in the .ibooks format generated using iBooks Author. ❞

What does this mean? Quite simply that if you intend to charge for your book you can *only* sell it through the Apple iBookstore unless you first export it in text or PDF format.

Is this fair? That depends on your point of view. If you had invested hundreds of pounds in buying Adobe InDesign or QuarkXPress and either of those companies said that you could only sell your printed products through its own online stores, you'd cry foul – as many are doing about the iBooks Author license terms. However, iBooks Author is free. It's purely a tool for producing books that work on Apple's mobile devices and nothing else, in which case you could argue that it is entirely logical that Apple should restrict the distribution of its output in the same way that it regulates the distribution of iPhone and iPad apps. They, too, are produced using free software – Xcode – that any member of Apple's developer community can download and use to earn themselves an income.

So long as you're willing to work with these limitations, there's simply no easier a way to make high quality, attractive, interactive books for the iPad, as we'll show you here.

Creating your first book

The first thing you'll see when you start iBooks Author is the Template Chooser (*below*). Although each of the templates appears to be designed for a specific kind of book – Botany, Astronomy, Entomology and so on – the more important distinction appears below each cover, where it describes the *kind* of book you can create with each one.

iBooks Author includes six high-quality templates to help you get started on the layout of your book.

As iBooks Author is intended to be used for creating textbooks, we're going to step away from *The Sketchbook of John, Constable* here and produce a book for first-time chicken-keepers, for which the 'Craft' style will be most appropriate as its layouts are quite folksy and very approachable.

iBooks Author creates a sample book of three pages with some placeholder text and images on each one. We'll swap these out for our own content in the process of building our book.

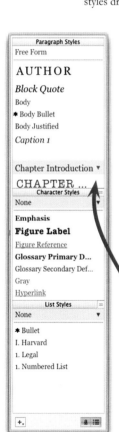

If you have ever used Keynote or Pages then the iBooks Author interface will already look very familiar. For those who have not used it, the toolbar's 'i' button (*left*) opens up the Inspector, which is where you'll do most of your formatting, as it gives you access to page, font and image settings.

At the opposite end of the toolbar is the pilcrow (it looks like a backwards P), which is traditionally used to mark the end of a paragraph. This opens the styles drawer (*below*).

Although you can format each item of text individually using the font, size and spacing drop-down selectors on the toolbar, you should get into the habit of using styles to format your content so that you keep a consistent style throughout your book, helping your readers to navigate the content and understand the various elements' hierarchical relationship to each other.

Adding and formatting content

The images and text that appear on the three sample pages are only placeholders, which you should swap out with your own content. At the moment they are only there to indicate the available boxes and to hold your styles. You can delete any that you don't want to use and resize them to fit a specific layout or the dimensions of their contents.

You can see the layout of the default first page of our chosen craft template on the previous spread, and how we have flowed in our own text on the next spread. You'll see that we have removed two

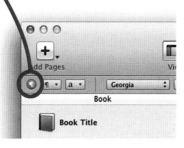

The pilcrow icon (*circled*) opens the style drawer which is used to organise and select the various saved styles associated with your document. You can also select styles directly using the pilcrow dropdown to the right of this toolbar button. The current active style is indicated by the down-pointing triangle and a highlight (in this case, *Chapter Introduction*).

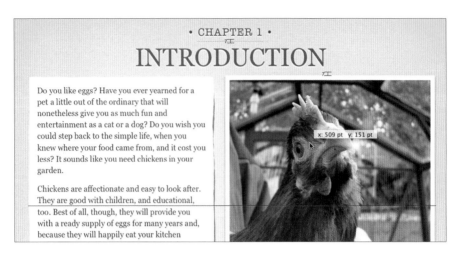

of the images, enlarged the one that remains and expanded the text box to match (see *facing page, top*).

It's easy to keep your elements in line with one another as you drag and resize them on the page, as iBooks Author throws up dynamic guidelines that show when you have aligned their centre points or set their spacings to match. In the example above, the horizontal blue like shows that the image of the chicken we are dragging within the image block is centred on the vertical axis as the horizontal centres of the box and image align. Further, the blue marks between the 'chapter 1' and 'introduction' line, and between 'introduction' and the image indicate that the spaces between each element are the same. Matching your spacing in this way creates a more balanced, pleasing layout. Further feedback is given in the pop-up coordinates that move with the pointer to show the image's precise position on the page.

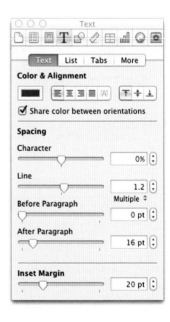

The Inspector

The Inspector (*right*) is where you'll make most of your choices. It's split into sections to cater for each part of your document (see *figure, facing page*), allowing you to make significant changes to every aspect of your document. Here we are using the Text Inspector to reformat our text.

Whenever you make a change in this way, it stops the selected text from conforming to its assigned style.

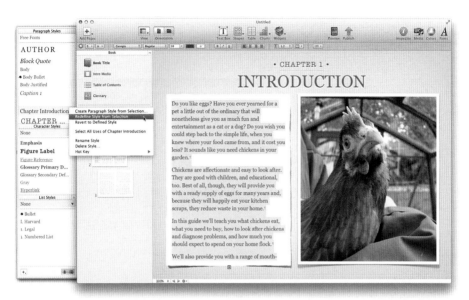

Although it does nothing to stop you from doing this, iBooks Author does throw up a warning in the shape of a red triangle beside the style name in the styles drawer (*left*). Clicking this calls up a menu through which you can tell it how to handle the aberration. If you want to preserve the original formatting so that you can reuse it, you would opt to '*Create Paragraph Style from selection*'. This would effectively preserve the original settings while allowing you to apply the new style again elsewhere.

However, we want to change the style itself, so on this occasion we are selecting '*Redefine Style From Selection*' (*above*). By changing the style in this way the current formatting will ripple through the rest of the document, with all other sections formatted in line with the same style. This is the power of working with styles: they are an efficient and effective timesaver when it comes to implementing changes to previously formatted text.

Now that we're happy with how the page looks we'll delete the other pages in the chapter by right-clicking the second page in the sidebar and selecting *Delete Section*. With this done we can now go on to perform a very important design process: handling what should happen when the iPad is rotated.

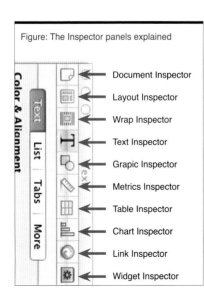

Figure: The Inspector panels explained

Document Inspector
Layout Inspector
Wrap Inspector
Text Inspector
Grapic Inspector
Metrics Inspector
Table Inspector
Chart Inspector
Link Inspector
Widget Inspector

Looking both ways

Because our book is so precisely designed, with positioned boxes, images and copy in the place of simple flowing text, we need to consider what will happen when our readers turn their iPad around from landscape to portrait orientation. As it stands, our book is only designed for use on a landscape display.

Click the toolbar's portrait orientation button (*right*) to switch to the alternate view and see how it affects your document. In our case it breaks our design. Our chicken image disappears and the text is left dangling off the bottom of the page. We need to fix this before we go any further.

We'll do this by copying the chicken image from the landscape layout by clicking back to it on the toolbar, selecting the image and using Command-C to copy it to the clipboard. Switching back to portrait we then use Command-V to paste it on the page. We now resize it and move it into its final position. As

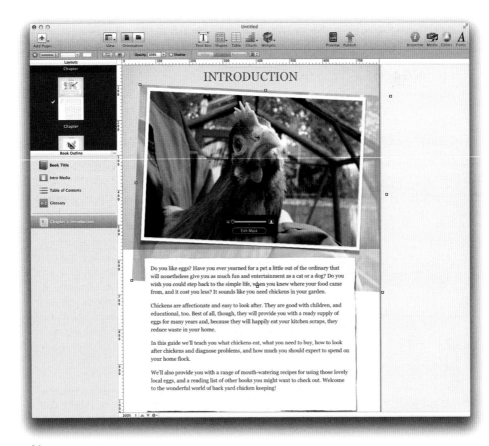

you can see from the image below, we have also rotated it slightly and are in the process of changing the size of its bounding box, having clicked *Edit Mask* to unlock its dimensions and then dragged the handles on each edge. Doing this also allows us to enlarge the image by using the slider.

Our first page is now complete, but before we go any further we should preview it in iBooks. To do this you'll need an iPad. Connect it to your Mac, start iBooks 2 and click *Preview* on the iBooks Author toolbar. Select your iPad in the dialogue box that drops down and the book will be compiled and sent to your device.

There won't be much to look at right now as we have only created a single-page document, but it's important to check that it works in both orientations by rotating the iPad through 90 degrees (*below*). Everything is working as we expected, so we can move on to the next part of our project.

Creating chapters

Our introduction is technically our first chapter, despite being just a single page. We now need to add chapters for our remaining content, each of which will be multi-page sections.

We do this by clicking *Add Pages | Chapter | Chapter*. iBooks Author drops a new untitled chapter into the sidebar, again consisting of a single page. If you're following along with your own copy of iBooks Author you'll immediately appreciate one of the limitations we discussed earlier: the fact that iBooks Author's limited palette of templates means your books can become quite samey without some extra input from yourself.

The new chapter that has been added to our book opens with the same layout as the introduction did before we started working on it. Fortunately, though, since we have made considerable changes to the layout of the introduction our readers shouldn't spot that. To make sure, we'll go further and redesign this chapter to give it a more appropriate layout, and a look and feel all of its own, first by amending this opening page, and then by tweaking the pages that follow.

Books designed in iBooks Author need to have both landscape and portrait formats defined to cater for a reader's rotated iPad.

Images appear in the sidebar when working in portrait mode.

Working with images

> used to home laid eggs from a flock with
> vegetables in its diet, you will not want to
> in the shop.
>
> Scraps can be thrown on the ground whe
> gladly take them up, although this can att
> if your chickens do not eat everything in
> ensure that any left-overs are tidied away
>
> It is far better, then, to give scraps in a de

Images really bring your work to life, not only breaking up the text so that reading it doesn't seem such a daunting prospect, but also helping to illustrate your points.

You can drag images into your layouts in either landscape or portrait mode, although the end result will be slightly different, depending on which method you choose.

Landscape mode

Drag in an image in landscape orientation and you can anchor it precisely by moving the blue dot (*above*) within the text. The text will reflow around it as you change its position. It should be noted, though, that an image's anchor position doesn't necessarily relate to its position on the page. You can independently move the image within the layout; the spot merely ties the image to your other content so that should the content be shunted onto another page as you change the copy the image reference will move with it.

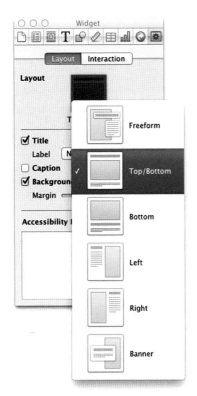

Portrait mode

In portrait mode, images are lined up in the sidebar. Once they've been transferred to the iPad, tapping these thumbnails opens larger versions in a new window. However, you can't position your images as precisely in this mode as you can in landscape mode, as they only ever line up with the references in the flowing text.

Placing your images in portrait mode adds a certain amount of further elements that aren't appended automatically when placing images in landscape mode, including a caption and figure reference. These are not added automatically when positioning them in landscape mode, but can be added by selecting the image in that orientation and opening the Widget Inspector (*left*).

Here, you can select whether or not to display the title above the image, the caption below it and a background behind it. Setting the margin dimensions lets you control how close the surrounding text comes to it when it's flowing around its edges.

Creating a cohesive product

As you flow in your text, iBooks Author creates as many pages as are required to contain it. By default these will be plain text pages, but you can drop images into them or change the underlying template by clicking the down-pointing arrow to the right of the page and selecting an alternative style (*right*).

Although the pages are arranged vertically in the sidebar, once they're transferred to an iPad your readers will move from one to the next by sweeping them to one side. The main editing window, therefore, arranges your pages in the same way. Should your monitor be large enough to allow it, drag out the iBooks Author window to display as many pages as you can (*below*) so that you can see how the pages interact with each other and ensure there are no jarring contrasts that will only manifest themselves as your readers navigate the finished book.

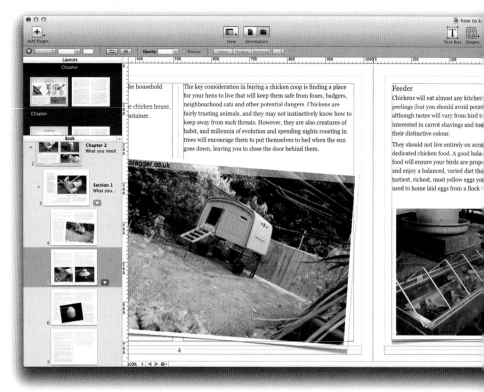

Gallery   Media

Review   Keynote

Interactive Image   3D

HTML

Working with widgets

So far you might be wondering why Apple was so sure that iBooks Author would revolutionise textbooks. It makes books easy to lay out, and produces attractive results, but until you start working with widgets other than plain images it isn't obvious what all the fuss is about.

There are seven different widgets to choose from, each of which helps to promote self-guided learning. They are largely self-explanatory, with *Media* handling video and audio, *3D* taking care or rotatable objects, and *Keynote* exposing a box in which you can place an existing Keynote presentation, allowing you to create slide-based content in Apple's answer to Microsoft PowerPoint and incorporate it in your book if you find this an easier way to work. We want to introduce an image gallery into our book, so we'll start by selecting Gallery from the Widgets menu.

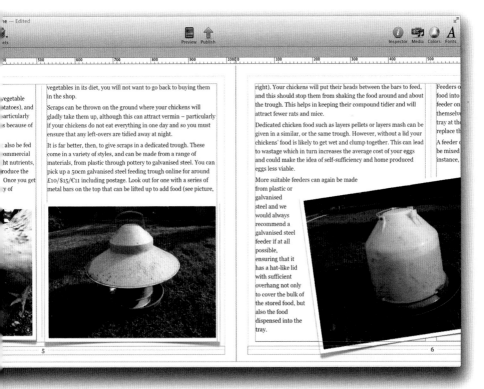

Every Widget can be customised courtesy of the Widget Inspector. We have positioned our Gallery widget at the end of the first chapter and selected *Top* from the list of layout options. This moves all of the associated titles and captions above the image itself and therefore positions the image immediately above the navigation dots. We've changed the label to *None* so that it doesn't prefix our title with a gallery reference, such as 'Gallery 2.1' (*below*).

That's the bare bones of our widget in place. However, it currently doesn't have any content. We need to add some pictures, which we do by switching to the Inspector's Interaction tab and using the '+' button to add images from the OS X file system (see *right*). We have added seven pictures, which is about perfect as it's not too many for our readers to wade through, but in reality you can add far more as the pane is a scrolling window.

The currently displayed image is indicated below the widget by a heavy spot. Should you prefer, you can replace these dots with thumbnails that switch out the images as your readers tap them. You can also change the order in which the images are presented by dragging the three bars that appear to the right of each one in the Gallery Media pane.

Each image needs an associated caption, which will be switched out in sync with the pictures as your audience taps through them. Click through each image in the Inspector's Gallery Media pane and replace the placeholder text on your page above it with the caption that explains its contents. This description can either repeat content from the main body of your work or add something new, but whatever you choose to put in that space you should bear in mind that any reader browsing through your book should be able to get something out of it without having read the rest of the spread on which it appears.

Every Widget can be customised to suit your needs by selecting options in the Widget Inspector. We have tweaked the position of the title and caption to place the image beside its navigation.

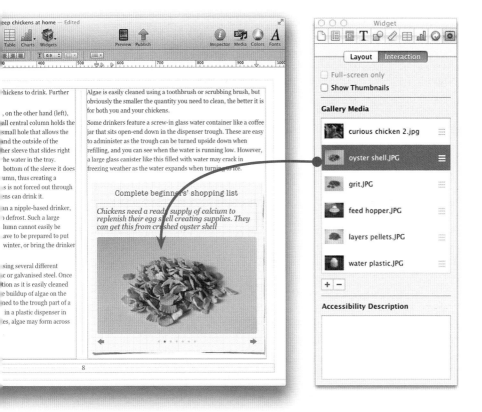

You should therefore, consider the caption to be an opportunity to present a summary of the text to which it relates, to lead the reader into the page. When your gallery appears in the finished book, those reading the book in landscape orientation can swipe through its various elements in situ (*below left*). Readers with a portrait-oriented iPad will find the gallery in the sidebar, like a regular image. Tapping there opens it full-screen and hides the rest of the book layout, allowing them to swipe in full-screen.

The Image Gallery is just one of the widgets on offer to editors working with iBooks Author. Despite the fact that it's fairly simple, doing no more than presenting images and captions, it is one of the many elements that won't translate well to regular ePub, and will have to be re-created as flat graphics for other platforms.

Building a glossary

If you are writing a technical manual, you should include a glossary of terms used throughout the book. iBooks 2 on the iPad has a specific Glossary entry in the navigation drop-down (*right*) through which your readers can find definitions of the terms you have used in your book. Glossary entries also pop up in any searches performed on the book's content.

The glossary is a special part of the book; scrolling to the top of the iBooks Author sidebar reveals this, the cover, opening media and contents page. Although you can tweak the contents manually, it is built automatically as you define various headings throughout your book. For the moment, then, we can ignore it.

Add each definition by clicking the '+' button in the sidebar and giving it a headword, then switch to the main body of the document and replace the placeholder text with your definition. Once you have defined several words you can start dragging related terms from the headwords column into the related area below your definition. These will be hyperlinked in the exported document

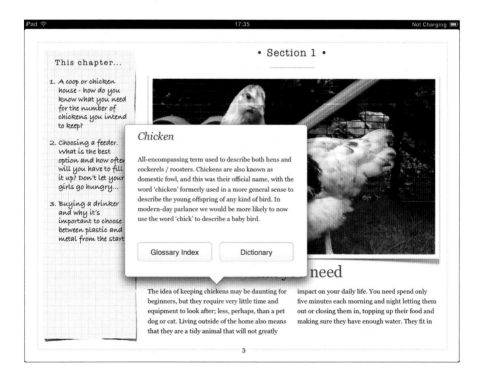

so that tapping on any one of them takes your reader to the linked definition without them having to enter the word using the keyboard.

If you're still in the throes of editing your book then you can cut some time here by building your glossary as you work your way through the book. Turn on the Glossary Toolbar (click *View | Show Glossary Toolbar* or press shift-command-E) and highlight the term you'd like to add to the glossary where it appears on your laid-out page. It will be automatically added to the Glossary toolbar, with an option to add it to the glossary at one end of the toolbar, and to link the word to an existing definition at the opposite end.

Choosing this latter option doesn't change the formatting of the word on the page, so decide whether you want to employ an easily recognised device along the same lines as a web hyperlink to indicate to your readers that tapping on the link will pop up a definition bubble (see *facing page*).

Publishing your iBooks Author product

It's important to keep saving and previewing your work on an iPad as you progress through your book so that you won't get to the end and find yourself presented with any nasty surprises. Once you have finished working on your layout and you're happy with the result it's time to think about how you want to make it available to the general public. You have three options here:

1. If you want to make a charge for it, click *Publish* on the iBooks Author toolbar to submit the book to the iBookstore. This will save a packaged version of the book that you can upload to the store using iTunes Producer. Bear in mind, though, that to go down this route you'll need an iBookstore seller account and an agreement in place covering your US tax obligations (even if you are located outside of the US, when you will want to opt out of having 30% tax deducted at source). You'll also have to create a sample of the book that your potential readers can download in advance of buying the complete product.

2. Export an iBooks file for loading onto an iPad to be read using iBooks 2 (click *File | Export*). Bear in mind that even though you're not going to be using the iBookstore the terms of the End User License Agreement still state that you can't sell the book, even through your own website.

3. Export the book as a series of PDF pages (again, *File | Export*) that can be opened in a regular application on any platform; in other words suitable for readers without an iPad. Since Apple updated its End User License Agreement, you can now sell books of this sort through other channels than the iBookstore.

Testing your eBook

You may think you're just writing a book, but you're not. What you're doing in self-publishing for an e-reading public is the same as app developers creating magazine or book applications for tablet computers and smartphones, albeit on a smaller, slightly less technical scale.

That means it's essential you test your product before either selling it through your own site (*see p106*) or uploading it to an online store (*see p90*). Not only is this good practice, allowing you to see exactly what your readers will find when they buy your book, but you'll also iron out any potential problems that could see it rejected during the approval phase of your submission to a store.

Testing for Kindle

Ideally you'd install your book on a hardware Kindle device and perform your tests by working your way through individual pages, skipping backwards and forwards between the chapters using the four-way controller, testing the hotlinks in the table of contents and changing the font size to check for any undesirable wrapping at larger sizes of those parts that should be kept on a single line.

However, without access to the full range of Kindle hardware devices and their tablet and smartphone app variants you can't be sure that a book that looks good on one will render properly on each of the others.

Fortunately Amazon has released a Kindle emulator for both Windows and the Mac as a free download from *http://amzn.to/yhWEL8*. This replicates the screen experience of viewing your compiled book on a Kindle Fire, 6in e-ink Kindle (Kindle, Kindle Touch and Kindle Keyboard), 9.7in Kindle DX, Kindle for iPad and Kindle for iPhone. The hardware buttons are replicated on the toolbar, and you can change the font size (although not the font face, which is always the default – Caecilia on the regular Kindle).

Run your books through this before uploading them to the store and you can confidently predict the experience your potential readers will have once they download your book, reducing the chances of you bring sent returns if you're selling your book through your own website, or earning yourself unfavourable reviews when selling directly through Amazon.

Testing ePub documents

Testing ePub documents is more complex than testing Kindle files as it is more difficult to predict which devices your audience will be using to access your work, and what those devices' capabilities will be. Where the Kindle is concerned, your priority should be to cater for 6in screen e-ink readers, followed by Kindle Fire users and then those with Kindle DX.

When it comes to ePub, though, how do you know whether you'd be better keeping iPad, Kobo or Nook users at the forefront of your calculations when compiling and testing your work. Sony Reader users? Those who might be reading on an Android or Windows Phone? And what of those using third-party ePub readers as extensions to their browser? Quite simply, you have to take a standards-based approach to ePub testing rather than testing for a specific, limited, closely defined platform.

Fortunately most electronic bookstores have standardised on ePub version 2.0 or later (at the time of writing, the most recently released update was ePub 3.0, shipped in October 2011). ePub is an open, published standard, against

Kindle Previewer emulates various different Kindle devices and iOS Kindle applications so you can see how your book will look on your readers' devices before submitting it to the store. Here we're testing our book using emulators for the Kindle Fire (left) and regular 6in e-ink-based Kindle devices.

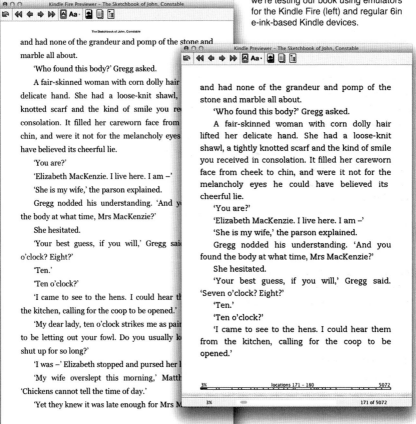

which it's easy to validate your files so that you can test for compilation glitches that could see it rejected during the upload and approval process.

This rejection will almost certainly come without warning and it may come without reason, too, leaving you trying to work out what was wrong. Fortunately EpubCheck can help.

Downloading and installing EpubCheck

EpubCheck is a Java application designed to be run from the command line, so don't expect any attractive interfaces. There is, however, limited drag and drop functionality on both Windows and the Mac.

You can find the latest stable build of EpubCheck at *http://bit.ly/AkkzQg*. Download the file marked 'binary', but don't download the later beta versions unless you have a very good reason as they might not always correctly validate your document.

You'll also need to check that you have Java installed on your system. Mac users can download the latest version for their OS through Software Update or by pointing their browser at *support.apple.com/ downloads* and searching for 'java', followed by their OS: *'java 10.5', 'java 10.6', 'java lion'* and so on. Windows users can download the latest update to Java from *java. com/getjava*.

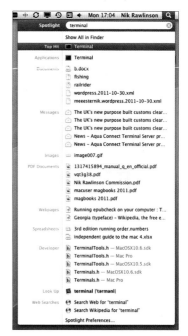

Whether you're using Windows or the Mac, EpubCheck is a Java application run from the command prompt.

Unzip the EpubCheck download and drag the complete folder inside the archive to your (Windows) Program Files or (Mac) Applications folder to complete the installation.

Testing your eBook

On the Mac, open Terminal, either from the Applications folder or Spotlight (*right*). On Windows, click Start and type *cmd.exe* in the 'Search programs and files' box (Windows 7) or 'Start Search' box (Windows Vista), and press return.

In both cases this launches the command prompt. If you've never seen it before, this is the text-based layer that underpins your graphical operating system – even though it is presented in a Windows or OS X application window – and often lets you more quickly access the operating system's core features than the graphical environment can, as well as running some non-native applications such as EpubCheck.

Make a note of the exact name of the version of EpubCheck you downloaded (in our case at the time of writing, it's epubcheck-1.2.jar) and type the following at the command line, replacing the name of the EpubCheck Java file and the ePub document with your own file names and without using any carriage returns or line breaks until the very end:

java -jar epubcheck-1.2.jar the-sketchbook-of-john-constable.epub

You'll need to direct Java to the exact location both of EpubCheck and the ePub you need to verify. To reduce the amount of typing you need do to, it therefore pays to locate them both in the same folder and to change to that folder before performing the test (on either operating system, use *cd* followed by a folder name to step down into it; to step up one level within the directory tree, swap the directory name for two dots, thus: *cd* ..).

If your book has been accurately compiled and complies with the ePub standards, you will see the message *No errors or warnings detected*. If you do, you can upload it to the various online stores with a high degree of confidence that it won't be rejected on technical grounds.

If you receive an error (even if it's only a warning), it's unlikely that your book will be accepted, so you'll need to make changes and compile it again. Among the most common errors is that reported by anyone who has tested their book by installing it on an iPad or iPhone, which requires synching it through iTunes. This can change some of the underlying metadata, indicating that there is a cover present, when there isn't. The specific error will run along the lines '*(iTunesMetadata.plist) exists in zip file, but is not declared in the OPF file*'. In this case, compile two versions of your file with different names and upload only one to your device for manual testing.

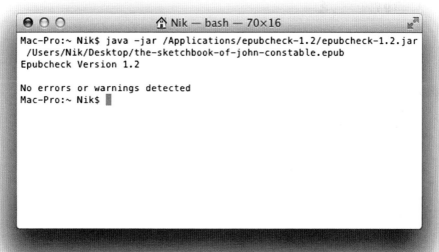

Chapter Four

Selling your eBook

Setting your book's price

Choosing a price isn't as simple as seeing what the competition charges and slightly undercutting them in the hope it'll bring in extra sales. It's a multi-part process that you need to complete for each store through which you choose to sell your book.

Learn from the pros

Barry Eisler landed himself a $500,000 publishing deal. He knew right away what he should do: he talked it over with his family, then turned it down.

Eisler isn't alone in turning his back on traditional publishing. A *New York Times* bestselling author, he's set himself up as a self publisher, convinced by a growing body of evidence that he'll earn more that way than any established imprint could pay him.

Eisler, like fellow author Joe Konrath, sees publishers' relevance diminishing in a rapidly-changing industry. 'We're the writers. We provide the content that is printed and distributed,' Konrath wrote in response to Eisler's comments. 'For hundreds of years, writers couldn't reach readers without publishers. We needed them. Now, suddenly, we don't. But publishers don't seem to be taking this Very Important Fact into account.'

The rise of eBooks, the US sales of which overtook paperbacks as far back as February 2011, is putting the old-school publishers out of their jobs – and their marketing departments, agents, and even bricks-and-mortar bookshops along with them – while ereaders like the Kindle and Kobo are helping novice authors to find an audience and make real money from writing.

Bypassing the print publishing cycle should lead not only to lower prices for the reader thanks to an increased level of competition between micro-publishers and a reduction in their overall costs as they don't need to invest in paper, ink and physically shipping books around the world, but also greater reader choice. For most people, their bestselling, groundbreaking first novel remains unwritten not because of the effort involved in getting the words on the page, but through lack of faith that those pages will ever be read. Imagine what might happen if publication were not a remote possibility, but a dead cert.

Signing a publishing contract is certainly something to celebrate, as it always has been, but it's no guarantee of success. Publishers make mistakes, just like the rest of us, pulping the 'next big thing' when it fails to find an audience, or passing up the chance to publish a blockbuster.

The publishing world is littered with stories of successful writers who were turned down time and time again when they were just starting out and trying to get overworked, time-short publishers to show some interest in their work. JK Rowling and Stephen King, both household names with millions of book sales behind them, went through the process of sending samples of their work to leading agents and publishing houses, only to receive a rejection slip in return.

Remember, though, that success comes through actually selling books, not simply through having a Penguin embossed on your cover. So, the more you sell, the greater your success, but how do you sell without a publisher? It isn't easy in print. The biggest sellers in any bookshop are stacked on the tables inside the door. Without a spot on the table, your chance of success is greatly diminished, but landing one is expensive.

That's where publishers are of greatest help to the first-time author. Bookshops can't afford to take a risk any more than a publisher can, and so often they will only stack books on these tables if they have already been heavily promoted in the press and proved themselves to be likely bestsellers, either because they've been written by well-known and successful names, or because the publisher has committed a significant budget to promoting the title. Without a publisher you won't be able to afford to compete with them, and so the shop-front table is almost certainly out of your reach. So, too, are the readers those tables attract.

There are no tables with eBooks. Publish on Kindle, or through Kobo or the iBookstore, and you'll be given the same virtual shelf space as Dan Brown, and probably earn better royalties. We can't speak with any certainty for Dan Brown, but most mainstream authors receive considerably less than 15% of the cover price for each book sold. You, on the other hand, can expect to earn up to 70% without any ongoing costs.

You'll also receive your payments sooner. Each of your sales is electronic, so it can be accurately registered right away.

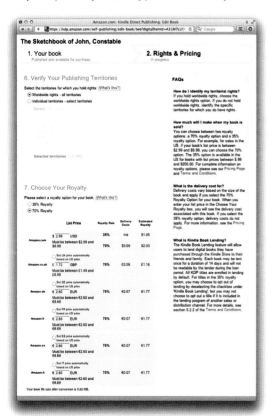

The Kindle Direct Publishing dashboard gives live feedback of your expected royalties at any price in each territory.

Although readers who buy a Kindle book by accident can return it for a refund if they haven't started reading it, the majority of your sales should progress to completion. The digital retailer will record the royalty against your account and, a few weeks later, you'll receive a cheque or bank transfer in exchange for your sales.

Compare that to the world of traditional publishing. It can easily take a year or more for a printed book to find an agent, several months for the agent to sell it, and a year to a year and a half for your publisher to edit, print and market it in line with their leisurely schedules. Your royalties will likely be paid every six to 12 months, so your chance of earning anything within three years of typing *The End* are very slim indeed. Can you afford to wait that long when you have other books waiting to be written?

Save yourself the frustration, sidestep the traditional publishing route, and you can be selling your book by next weekend. You'll have a three-year head start on your print-based rivals in which to start writing a sequel and beyond. First, though, you need to settle on a realistic price.

Selling through Amazon

The first step in selling your work through the Kindle store is choosing the territories in which the book should be sold and what royalties you'd like to earn. The standard share is 35% of the cover price, but if you price your book between £1.49 and £6.99 and enable lending you can hike it to a very generous 70% in the UK and US. See below the thresholds to which each royalty band applies, and note that although it must be enabled to qualify for 70% royalties, it's not currently possible for readers outside of the US to borrow and lend books with other Kindle users.

Think back to what we said earlier here: by following the traditional publishing route you would be lucky to earn royalties of around 15% on net receipts – ie wholesale prices, after discounts of 50% or more have been given to retailers as an inducement to take your book. On a £7.99/$7.99 book, then, even

	Royalty rate	Minimum price	Maximum price
US dollars	35%	$0.99	$200
	70%	$2.99	$9.99
British pounds	35%	£0.75	£120
	70%	£1.49	£6.99
Euros	35%	€0.86	€173.91
	70%	€2.60	€8.69

Table: The bands within which you must price each book to qualify for each royalty rate.

if you swing royalties of 15%, you might earn 59p/59c. From this, your agent would also take a cut of 10% to 15%.

Sell your book for £1.99/$2.99 on Kindle, on the other hand, and you can opt for 70% royalties, which will earn you £1.39/$2.09 per copy while still significantly undercutting the mainstream publishers and increasing your chance of a sale. Reduce your price yet further to the lowest level at which you'd qualify for 70% royalties, and you'd still earn over £1/$2 for each copy sold, while encouraging readers to buy a copy of your book because it's such a bargain when compared to mainstream novelists' work.

Don't believe us? There's plenty of evidence that it works.

Novelist Joe Konrath was selling his book, The List, for $2.99. Through the first two weeks of February 2011 it sold an average of 43 copies a day, each of which earned him royalties of 70%, pulling in $87 daily. On the 15th of the month, he dropped the price to just 99 cents – a level that is eligible for royalties of only 35% – and sales increased massively. It went from being the 1078th best-selling charged-for book in the Kindle Store to 78th. Daily sales increased to 533 copies, and although the amount of money earned by each one fell from $2.03 to just 35 cents, his average daily earnings now stood at $187. Dropping the price – and the royalties – has more than paid for itself in his case.

Amazon will 'deliver' your book electronically for free if you opt for 35% royalties, but if you choose 70% it will charge you 10p (UK) or 15 cents (US and Canada) per megabyte to send it to your readers. The size of the book is calculated when you upload it, and the charge worked out pro-rata to the nearest kilobyte. So, a book that weighs in at 200KB would cost 2p or 3 cents to deliver, depending on territory, which would be deducted from your royalties.

Although words and numbers don't consume a great deal of either storage space or bandwidth when delivered, images are considerably more space-hungry, which is why comparatively few highly illustrative books have traditionally been converted for sale through the Kindle store. This is because they must each be encoded and embedded within the book, and is the reason why the timeline graphics that we used when formatting *The Sketchbook of John, Constable*, were kept very simple and rendered in just one colour.

Kindle cost conversion

By default, Amazon will convert your chosen dollar price for your book to work out what it will cost anyone who is shopping in the UK or a European Amazon store unless you specify a bespoke price for each market. Note, though, that if you do it then it could have further reaching consequences than you expected.

Setting different euro prices for the French, German, Spanish and Italian stores means that Amazon will always choose the lowest of these when selling to other European customers who reside outside of those territories. So, for example, if you set €2.99 for French customers and €3.99 for those shopping from Germany, anyone buying your book in Switzerland, to whom Amazon allows sales from both its French and German stores, will see it advertised at €2.99 – the price set for France.

Likewise, if you choose a UK price of £1.49 and a US price of $5.99, any UK customers shopping at Amazon.com will see your book priced, at the time of writing when $1 = 64p, at $2.30. Unless you have any good and specific reasons for setting particular prices in different markets, therefore, our advice would be to set a price in your home market and for Amazon.com, and allow the system to work out what to charge elsewhere.

Selling through other stores

Amazon is the easiest store for first-time publishers to get their books into. The whole process is largely automated and once you have set up your account (see the section *Uploading your book*) you don't need to provide much in the way of tax forms and business identification documents.

The price at which your book appears in online stores (here, the Apple iBookstore) is likely to differ from the price you set in your aggregator (see right).

Should you wish to sell through other leading stores – and in particular Apple's iBookstore – you are often better served setting up your account through an aggregator (see table, below).

Each of these has different policies and practices and offers different levels of revenue share. LibreDigital, for example, pays 55% of the revenue received from Apple, which itself is 70% of the sale price of your book, keeping 45% for

	Address	Region
Ingram	*ingramcontent.com*	North America
INscribe Digital	*ingrooves.com*	North America
LibreDigital	*libredigital.com*	North America
Lulu	*lulu.com*	North America
Smashwords	*smashwords.com*	North America
Bookwire	*bookwire.de*	Europe
Immaterial	*immateriel.eu*	Europe

Table: Global eBook aggregators. Source: Apple / bit.ly/zN0yu0

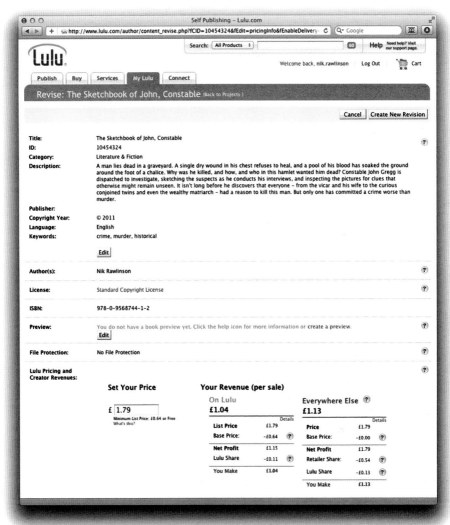

Like Amazon, Lulu displays a dynamically updated breakdown of the revenue you can expect to receive from sales of your book. Note that profits from third-party stores (here called 'Everywhere Else') is higher than from Lulu itself, despite Lulu taking a cut of the profit. This is because you don't need to pay the Base Price, which covers Lulu's hosting costs – in this instance 64p per book per sale.

itself to cover the cost of its services. However, you may have to wait for your payment. Apple sends payments to LibreDigital up to 45 days after the end of the month in which you make a sale. LibreDigital will then make a payment to you 30 days later.

So, if you sold a book on 1 January Apple might not pay LibreDigital until 17 March. LibreDigital would then pay you on 17 April, 108 days after you sold the book. Further, it will only make that payment if it has collected $500 of revenue on your behalf, meaning that if your share of revenue from the iBookstore is only $50 a month it will take over 11 months (allowing for the 30-day payment turn-around) for you to receive your first cheque.

In reality, it will take longer, as that $500 is comprised of your 55% cut. The revenue delivered from the iBookstore required to achieve this is $909 after Apple takes its own 30% cut. Raw sales, then, need to reach $1300 before you can expect payment.

This sounds slow when compared to Amazon's payment schedule, under which you can expect to receive payment 60 days following the end of the month in which you make your sale, so long as you have accrued sales of at least $10.

Lulu, meanwhile, offers an 80% / 20% split of revenues received after the retailer – the iBookstore, for example – has taken its cut, which is typically 30% of the asking price. Lulu keeps only the smaller portion of that split for itself, and also offers the option of publishing print-based books using the same content as you are publishing online.

Lulu has two payment options. The traditional cheque-based route requires that you have at least $20 waiting for payment, in which case it will send you your remuneration within 45 days of the end of each quarter. Lulu's quarters end on the 15th or February, May, August and November.

However, if you have a PayPal account then you can both speed up the turn-around and lower the threshold that triggers a payment. Follow this route and you'll receive payments monthly for all account balances of $5 or more. You can also choose the currency in which you receive payment, from US dollars, British pounds or euros.

eBook sales and tax

They may have no physical form, but digital books attract tax. The way they are handled differs from country to country.

Value Added Tax (VAT) and Sales Tax

If you're publishing in the UK then bear in mind when setting your pricing that Customs and Excise counts eBooks as 'services' (the service being the act of serving the download), and as services attract VAT this will also apply to your downloaded eBook.

If you're selling books for the Kindle market, Amazon adds this to your asking price using the rate charged in Luxembourg at the time of purchase. At the time of writing this stands at 15%, so if you're looking to hit the magical 99p price point you'll actually have to price your book at just 86p. From this you'll earn 30p per copy. At this price you'll either need to sell a lot of copies to make it worth your while, or be writing and publishing books for fun and satisfaction.

Sales through the EU Kindle stores, settled in euros, attract VAT of just 3%.

The same is true of Apple's iBookstore and the various eBook aggregators. Lulu, for instance, charges sales tax in the United States based on the shipping address of the downloaded book (which is deemed to be the credit card address if no alternative is provided). In Canada it will apply at the very least Goods and Services Tax (GST) and possibly also Provincial Sales Tax (PST) or Harmonisation Sales Tax (HST), depending on the province in which the customer resides. In the European Union it applies VAT 'on all applicable goods or services delivered to destinations in those member countries where thresholds have been met'.

Tax registration

Fortunately much of the complexity of collecting and paying over tax is handled by your book retailer, freeing you up to get on with writing and publishing more books, but if you want to sell in the US you will usually need to provide documentation that proves your tax status, as royalty payments are taxable income, in the same way as a salary, self-employed earnings and bank interest.

US self-publishers will need to provide their personal tax number. If they are publishing through their own company, and that company will receive the revenues from each sale, then they should instead supply their business tax number. For individuals publishing in the US, this is done using IRS form W-9.

Publishers based outside of the United States will need to complete documentation from the Internal Revenue Service that indicates that the tax they are due to pay will be collected in their resident country, so long as that country has signed an income tax treaty with the US. If not, 30% of all earned revenues will be withheld to meet US tax demands from foreign entities.

Form W-8BEN registers foreign entities as non-eligible US tax payers. It is available on the IRS site at *irs.gov* (search for '*w-8ben*' for the most recently-published edition) and on completion should be forwarded to the publishing agent, store or aggregator handling the sales of your books on your behalf. This will exempt them from withholding the 30% tax on your revenue, allowing them to pay you the gross amount collected.

Tax return

How you account for your digital earnings will differ from case to case. If you are publishing as a company they will obviously form part of your corporate income and so will have to pass through your books, at which point they will attract corporation tax or equivalent. For personal publishers it is an add-on to salaried or freelance income and will need to be accounted for on your end of year tax return.

Designing your cover

There's no such thing as a cover on a digital book – merely an embedded image that's given elevated status and displayed on some ereader home screens. Amazon's Kindle Fire and the various Kobo readers both use them as icons through which you select the book you want to read; regular e-ink based Kindles use plain text menus, with 'covers' only displayed when you specifically select them from the *Go To* menu.

Nonetheless, if you were to pay for assistance in the production of any part of your book, we would suggest the cover second only to professional editing services. Why? Because it will also appear on the various online stores selling your book. After the title, it's most likely the first thing your potential customers look at when they click your book in the list of available titles.

If you choose not to upload an image of your own design, Amazon will instead use a placeholder image, which is unlikely to reflect your book's contents.

Keep it simple

When designing a cover it is essential that you keep size at the front of your mind. Covers in Amazon's general listings are around 100 pixels tall (the width is proportional), while those on a book's dedicated page are 240 pixels tall. Create a file of those proportions in an image editor and you'll see how cramped a complex design will appear.

If you are going to use any imagery on the cover it therefore needs to be bold, striking and simple. Avoid complex, fine detail that will be lost when Amazon shrinks down your image to these sizes, and be sure to leave space for your title and author name. This need not be a blank, white area, though; often, an area of flat detail, such as a sky, skin or grass makes a suitable backdrop.

Be bold

Your book title will appear beside its cover image, but many readers will expect to see it on the artwork itself. A bare image without any words on it looks like an illustration or placeholder graphic rather than a cover.

Here, too, you need to consider the size of the cover thumbnail. If your readers can't make out every word on the cover, that's not a problem, but very long book titles will lend themselves better to purely typographic covers, rather than those in which the words are forced to fit around the image.

Be careful when selecting colours so that the background is neither lost (green text on grass/blue text over a bright sky), nor conflicting. Some colour

You need to make a big impact within a small space when designing your cover. Amazon's default height for covers in its category pages (*above*) is just 100 pixels; on books' dedicated pages it's 240 pixels (*right*).

combinations, such as red on purple and yellow on green, are uncomfortable to read. Although you're not asking your potential customer to consume the whole of your book in that combination, poor colour choices in your cover design can fundamentally affect its impact. Pink text on an SAS thriller, or a blood-dripping gothic font on a love story, for example, would both be poor choices.

Bear in mind that on the e-ink Kindles your cover will be rendered in greyscale, so ensure there is a strong contrast between your background and any text you use.

Quality and format

Amazon accepts either Jpeg or Tif image files, which are uploaded through the Kindle Direct Publishing dashboard when setting up your new book. Despite being shrunk down when used in listings, each must be at least 500 x 800 pixels, but wherever possible 2000 pixels on the longest size. Usually this would be the spine height, as Amazon states an ideal proportion of 1:1.6, which would make a 2000-pixel tall cover 1250 pixels wide.

Save your image in RGB (Red, Green, Blue) format at the highest possible colour depth. On a PC this will usually be expressed at 16 million colours; on a Mac, 'Millions of colours'.

Uploading your book

With your book written and compiled into a compatible eBook format, you're ready to upload it to the store of your choice. Certainly we would recommend at the very least submitting your book to Amazon using Kindle Direct Publishing as it is one of the easiest and quickest routes to a potential audience. We'll walk you through that process here.

However, you shouldn't ignore the services of the various aggregators that will submit ePub books to a wide range of online stores, allowing you to reach the largest possible market. Bear in mind, though, what we said about the payment intervals of the various aggregators and the stores they supply (see *Choosing a price*) and choose the one that offers the fastest turn-around at the lowest threshold so that you can start earning money as soon as possible. Bear in mind, too, that many outlets rule that you must not sell the same book cheaper through its competitors.

Kindle Direct Publishing

Log in to the Kindle Direct Publishing Dashboard at *http://kdp.amazon.com* using your regular Amazon account details. Before you can sell books through

Use the Description section of the book-processing dashboard to write an engaging summary of your work. Don't give away the ending, but do feed the reader sufficient information to pique their interest Double-check your spelling and grammar, remembering at all times that this should act as a sales and promotion tool for your work.

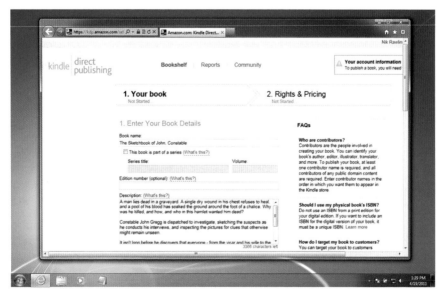

the online store you'll need to agree to Amazon's terms and conditions. You will also see a warning in the top corner of the Dashboard screens (*opposite*) warning you that your account information is incomplete. Click it and enter your address and how you'd like to be paid. You'll have to wait until you hit £100 / $100 / €100 of sales, depending on territory, if you want to be paid by cheque, but if you're happy to accept an electronic funds transfer (EFT) straight into your bank account, Amazon will make a payment for every £10 / $10 / €10 earned. You'll need to choose cheque or EFT for each of the territories in which Amazon sells electronic books, but bear in mind that while euro-based sales can be paid in dollars, British pounds or euros, sales in the US can only be paid in dollars, regardless of where your bank account it held, while royalties for sales made in the UK can be settled in dollars or pounds. Once you have agreed to the

When selecting the price of your book you can choose different levels for each of the territories in which Amazon sells Kindle books. Bear in mind that while setting low prices may induce increased sales it will take you longer to reach the payment threshold. If you have confidence in your work, consider trialling a price that could cross the payment threshold with one sale.

terms and conditions and entered your address and account details you can start the publishing process.

Return to your bookshelf and click *Add a new title*. Work your way through the publishing form, at the very least giving a title, language and author name, as well as a description of up to 4,000 characters (*see opposite page*). This is the blurb that appears on the book's listings page, both on the Amazon web pages and the store pages accessed directly through the Kindle, so think carefully about what you write here and come up with something that showcases your work. Double-check your spelling.

Amazon needs to know where to file your book in its catalogue by specifying the categories under which it should be filed. You'll need to select the two most relevant options, and at the same time type in your own descriptive tags to improve search performance.

Amazon sells public domain books and those for which copyright applies, and requires all publishers to specify into which camp their book falls. Public domain books can still be charged for regardless of your lack of involvement but only ever attract royalties of 35%.

It's up to you whether or not you upload a cover image, but we'd strongly recommend it. See our guidance in the previous section for designing your cover. If you don't supply one, Amazon will use a flat placeholder that will do little to sell your work. Remember, the key thing to keep in mind when working your way through these screens is that everything you do should help to entice readers and generate more sales – and thus more revenue – for you. A well-designed cover image is a key part of this.

Ensure that whatever image you choose it is saved using the RGB (Red, Green, Blue) colour space, rather than CMYK (Cyan, Magenta, Yellow, black), is at least 500 pixels wide and no more than 1,280 pixels tall. If your background is white, add a 3-pixel wide grey border to help it stand out on the Amazon listing pages. This cover image isn't the same as the one that forms part of your book: that's embedded within the eBook file itself, so can be optimised for the Kindle.

Still with us? Good. You're almost there.

Finally, you need to decide whether you want to enable Digital Rights Management (DRM) and then upload your actual book file.

Digital Rights Management is a way in which your book can be encoded such that it can't be passed on from one reader to another, except in line with Amazon's usual rules about loaning books for a short, specified period. You can't change your mind on the DRM issue once you've published your book, so think very carefully whether you're happy for people to share your work without making any further payments to yourself before going beyond this point.

Amazon will check your uploaded file and, assuming it meets its requirements, will let you complete the publishing process. This involves choosing the territories in which the book should be sold and what royalties you'd like to earn.

Amazon Approval

Because of the approval process involved, it usually takes Amazon two working days to publish an English language book, after which the Dashboard's Reports section will show your earnings week by week.

It takes longer to publish in foreign languages, so plan ahead and don't leave things until the last moment. If you need to meet a particular deadline plan ahead and be prepared to have your book on the digital shelves a little earlier than required so that you don't risk missing potential sales.

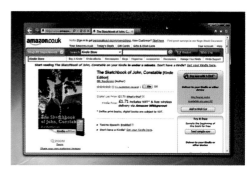

It takes around two days for Amazon to approve an English language book, and longer for foreign books. However, once it has completed the process it appears on Amazon's various national stores in the same format as books produced by big-name publishing houses.

Why it could pay to ignore everyone but Amazon

Amazon is pushing hard to become the only outlet that self-publishers – and traditional publishers – consider for their eBooks, and thus drive sales of its Kindle hardware readers.

In exchange for making your book available as part of the Kindle Owners' Lending Library, assigning them US rights and selling them exclusively on Amazon's Kindle Store for at least 90 days, you can choose to enrol it in KDP Select. The Kindle Owners' Lending Library is currently only available in the US to Amazon Prime members, a month's membership of which is included in the purchase of every Kindle Fire.

KDP Select is a monthly fund distributed pro rata among all enrolled members on the basis of the number of times their published book was borrowed by Amazon Prime members, each of which can borrow one book a month for as long as they choose. This is distinct from Kindle Lending, in which US users can lend books they have purchased to other Kindle users.

The maths behind KDP Select is quite simple. As Amazon puts it:

> ...if the monthly fund amount is $500,000, the total qualified borrows of all participating KDP titles is 100,000, and your book was borrowed 1,500 times, you will earn 1.5% (1,500/100,000 = 1.5%), or $7,500 for that month.

Amazon is currently announcing the size of the shared fund on a monthly basis, on the 25th of the preceding month, but for guidance has stated that the annual total currently stands at a minimum of $6m. In line with this it has been offering a combined monthly fund of $500,000, although this may increase if there is a sudden influx of new participants. Amazon has stated that it will continually review the size of the fund 'to make participation in KDP Select a compelling option for authors and publishers'.

Don't sign up for KDP Select without first considering your options. In agreeing to distribute your digital book exclusively through KDP, you are entering into an agreement not only to remove it from all competing stores, but also from your website or blog, whatever its digital format – including PDF, plain text, Microsoft Word and so on. You also can't get around the issue by adding bonus chapters to the Amazon offering while continuing to sell an unexpanded edition of the book elsewhere. If you have made physical copies or an audiobook version, however, it would not preclude you from continuing to sell these online.

Combined with the ease of publishing, the lack of any need for an intermediate aggregator and Amazon's fast turn-around when it comes to paying royalties, this makes signing up to Amazon exclusively a particularly tempting proposition.

Setting up your own publishing imprint

Why might you want to set up your own publishing house when it's just as easy to self-publish under your own name or use the services of Lulu and co to publish under their brands?

For some it's a matter of pride. The idea of self-publishing still has a suspicious smell about it, largely due to the number of so-called vanity publishers, some of whom will put out anyone's work regardless of talent (or otherwise) in exchange for a fee. Further, quality control is often slim to non-existent in self-published work. Without a team of proof-readers, fact-checkers and layout artists, a self-published book is the work of just one person, end to end. That person is often so close to the book in question that they are unable to view it dispassionately, and so won't spot obvious mistakes, and may choose to let through sub-standard work.

Readers can spot shoddy work within the first few pages, and few reviewers would ever consider giving a self-published book space in their august publications. Bookshops, too – particularly large chains – will be reluctant to give over shelf space to an unproven self-published author when they could instead devote it to authors published under a recognised imprint.

Setting up your own publishing operation won't make your writing any better, so don't expect the extra layer of legitimacy it affords to make your readers any more forgiving of substandard work, but it may be enough to make someone who otherwise wouldn't ever pick up a self-published work consider your book.

Products that qualify for ISBNs

- Books with textual content
- Electronic products such as CDs, downloads, audiobooks, that have textual and / or instructional content
- Journals published more frequently than once a year
- Sets of volumes or packs of books or electronic products with a textual and / or instructional content

Source: Nielsen BookData

Registering as a publisher

Every properly published book needs to be catalogued using an ISBN – an International Standard Book Number – to be efficiently catalogued. This uniquely identifies both the book and its publisher, and is used as a global publishing standard with which retailers can order stock. Without an ISBN they won't be able to buy printed editions of your book – if you choose to produce them – and many digital retailers, including Apple's iBookstore, won't stock it. There is no legal requirement to obtain an ISBN when publishing your work, but it will greatly increase its saleability if you do – particularly if you want to publish in those territories, such as China, where it is obligatory to display an ISBN barcode on your book.

Aggregators like Lulu will assign you an ISBN from their own pool if you choose to publish under their own imprint, but with Lulu being such a well-known self-publishing outlet this doesn't do much to disguise the fact that you're publishing your own book. You may therefore decide to register your own ISBN numbers.

In the UK and Republic of Ireland this is handled by Nielsen BookData (*nielsenbookdata.co.uk*); in the US it's handled by Bowker (*myidentifiers.com*). Each requires that you register as a publisher before buying your first set of ISBNs. The process differs slightly in each instance.

Registering as a publisher in the UK and Republic of Ireland

You don't need to be a registered company to register as a 'publisher', as Nielsen regards a publisher simply as 'the person or body who takes the financial risk in making a product available', and clarifies:

> ...if a product went on sale and sold no copies at all, the publisher is usually the person or body who loses money. If you get paid anyway, you are likely to be a designer, printer, author or consultant of some kind.

So, if you're risking anything with greater fiscal value than your professional reputation, in all likelihood you're eligible to register as a publisher.

When you first register you can choose between an initial batch of 10, 100 or 1000 ISBNs alongside your publisher prefix. At £118.68, £256.32 and £652.32 respectively (including VAT), this makes the 1000 number deal by far the best value, but it represents a considerable investment for a first-time publisher who may take several years to use up the larger allocation. Note, however,

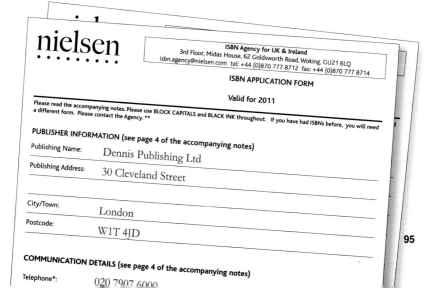

nielsen

ISBN Agency for UK & Ireland
3rd Floor, Midas House, 62 Goldsworth Road, Woking, GU21 6LQ
isbn.agency@nielsen.com tel: +44 (0)870 777 8712 fax: +44 (0)870 777 8714

ISBN APPLICATION FORM

Valid for 2011

Please read the accompanying notes. Please use BLOCK CAPITALS and BLACK INK throughout. If you have had ISBNs before, you will need a different form. Please contact the Agency. **

PUBLISHER INFORMATION (see page 4 of the accompanying notes)

Publishing Name: Dennis Publishing Ltd

Publishing Address: 30 Cleveland Street

City/Town: London

Postcode: W1T 4JD

COMMUNICATION DETAILS (see page 4 of the accompanying notes)

Telephone*: 020 7907 6000

How to decode an ISBN

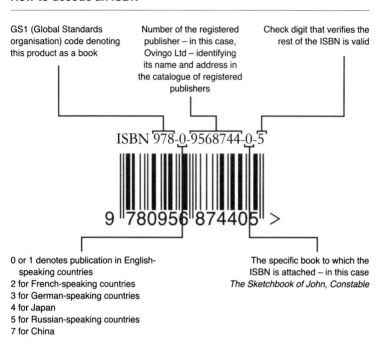

GS1 (Global Standards organisation) code denoting this product as a book

Number of the registered publisher – in this case, Ovingo Ltd – identifying its name and address in the catalogue of registered publishers

Check digit that verifies the rest of the ISBN is valid

ISBN 978-0-9568744-0-5

0 or 1 denotes publication in English-speaking countries
2 for French-speaking countries
3 for German-speaking countries
4 for Japan
5 for Russian-speaking countries
7 for China

The specific book to which the ISBN is attached – in this case *The Sketchbook of John, Constable*

that as you can only use each ISBN once, you can't put the same one on two different versions of a single book, so if you were to produce separate ePub and Mobipocket versions of your title you would immediately use up two of your ISBNs.

Fortunately, much of that initial price covers your first registration and not only the issuance of your ISBNs. Should you need to expand your batch of allocated number in the future, therefore, you need only pay for the numbers themselves. Pre-registered publishers can buy a further ten, 100 or 1000 ISBNs for £66.36, £204 and £600 respectively.

ISBNs are issued by email in an attached Excel spreadsheet, usually within ten working days. If you've left things until the last minute you can expedite the process by paying an additional £62.40, cutting the processing time to three working days. A further £24 will buy you a printed and posted record of your order if you buy 100 or 1000 numbers. This latter service is not available on orders of ten ISBNs. The same conditions apply for both newly registering and pre-registered publishers.

ISBN application forms can be downloaded from *bit.ly/zC4aNj* and must be posted or faxed back to Nielsen for processing. Applications can't be made online or sent by email. When you receive your numbers, take care of them, as a charge will be made to re-issue your allocation.

Registering as a publisher in the US

In the US, it's possible to buy a single ISBN for $125, ten for $250, 100 for $575 and 1000 for $1000. As we pointed out in the UK section, above, you will need to apply a different ISBN to every format in which you choose to publish your book, so even if you're putting out just two editions – ePub and Mobipocket – it makes sense to immediately buy a block of ten numbers, as it costs the same as just two and builds in a degree of future-proofing to your nascent publishing operation.

Bowker defines a publisher along very similar lines as Nielsen, as 'a person or firm whose business is the publishing of books or other publications to which an ISBN can be assigned, and includes e-book publishers, audio cassette and video producers, software producers and museums and associations with publishing programs'. The process is slightly easier, though, as it can be completed online at *myidentifiers.com/?q=createAccount*

Books and barcodes

Barcodes will only be of interest if you choose to produce printed editions of your book. Books traditionally display EAN (European Article Number) barcodes that translate their ISBN into machine-readable form, allowing them to be scanned at checkouts and during stock control. In the US, this is usually presented in the form of a "Bookland" barcode, which presents the traditional ISBN (*see p96*) with a price-derived barcode beside it. This second barcode, which is smaller than the ISBN barcode, sits to the right of the scanned area. It consists of five digits and is referred to as an EAN-5.

The first digit of the code denotes the currency in which it is priced. 0 and 1 denote British pounds; 3 is used for Australian dollars; 4 for New Zealand dollars; 5 for US dollars and 6 for Canadian dollars. The four digits that follow it represent the price, without a decimal point, so 51099 would be used on a book priced at US $10.99.

The standard location for a Bookland EAN is the lower-right corner of the rear cover. Wherever possible the ISBN portion of the barcode should be presented at 2 x 1.25in; the price part at 1.75 x 1in. Use black, dark blue or dark green to print the barcodes, on red, yellow or white backgrounds to ensure they stand out adequately (black on white is best). For more information about presenting Bookland EAN barcodes, check out *myidentifiers.com/barcode/faqs*

Chapter Five

After Publication

Promoting yourself in Amazon Author Central

Author Central is Amazon's quasi social network for authors and their readers. If you are the author of any book listed in Amazon's catalogue, you're eligible to sign up, and use the Author Central service to promote your work.

Amazon has produced localised editions of Author Central for US and UK users at *authorcentral.amazon.com* and *authorcentral.amazon.co.uk* respectively, each of which you can sign in to using your regular Amazon account credentials. Here we'll be working our way through setting up our presence via the UK URL, as our account is registered with Amazon.co.uk.

Signing up to Author Central

Once you've signed in to Author Central, Amazon searches its catalogue for books it believes you have written. Here it's found two out of the 19 books listed in its catalogue for Nik Rawlinson. We'll need to add the other books when our account has been confirmed, but for the moment we'll click the *Yes, this is me* link (*below*). Amazon now sends a confirmation email to our registered email address which, once clicked to return to Author Central, confirms our credentials and completes the sign-up process. We can now start populating our account.

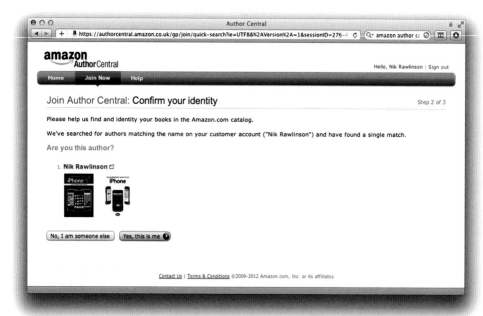

Adding books to your record

If, like us, Amazon missed some of your books when setting up your account, you'll need to add them manually. Click the *Books* tab on the menu that runs across the top of Author Central, followed by *Add more books*.

Fortunately the process is largely automated, with Amazon finding a further 16 titles under the name Nik Rawlinson (*above*). In this case, each of these is correct, so we only need click the buttons below each one to confirm them and add them to our profile. Unfortunately the process isn't always instantly completed, and it can take up to five days for a book to appear in your bibliography (in our experience it's actually much quicker). In this case they'll be listed as 'Coming Soon' on the books tab page, so you can see Amazon is still working on it.

Don't be tempted to try and fool the system by claiming to have written books that you haven't. Here we have tried to add a book that we legitimately penned, but which has been submitted to Amazon by the publisher under the name of a magazine – MacUser (*left*).

Amazon has recognised the mismatch between our account name and that attached to the book, and won't let us add it to our account without some further explanation, either by adding a pen name or getting in touch directly.

Tell your readers about yourself

As a first-time digital publisher, it's unlikely your readers will know anything about you unless you have become known in another field already. Readers may be reluctant to buy your books – in particular, non-fiction works – if they aren't convinced that you're qualified to be writing and publishing in the first place.

The Author Central biography (*below*) is your chance to add a short introduction about yourself that would act as a sales tool for your own personal brand in the same way that your book descriptions are a sales tool for each individual work.

The key here is to keep things snappy. Amazon suggests being creative by sharing the kind of anecdotes you might be asked to relate on a talk show should you ever be interviewed about your work. Don't exaggerate or you're liable to be found out, which won't do much to promote future sales and, as we stressed

Your biography is the most useful tool Amazon offers to inroduce yourself to potential readers. Think of it as the personal equivalent of the summary that accompanies a book.

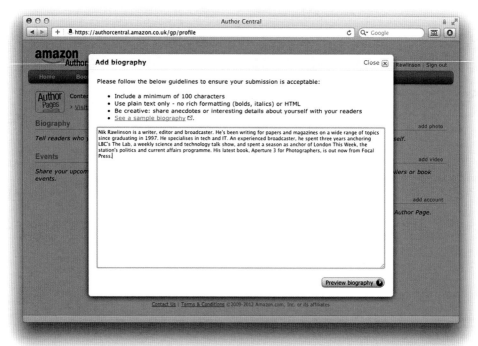

in the section 'Uploading Your Book', double-check all of your spelling and grammar. In most instances this biography will be your readers' first chance to learn more about you, so it's important that you create a good first impression if you want to convince them to spend money on your products.

You should review your biography regularly to keep it fresh and current. Talk about your life outside of writing and don't be afraid to name-check recent releases, which again should give you something to update at regular intervals.

Add a photo

You can't fail to notice, when looking at stacks of magazines in your local newsagent, how many of their covers feature a person's face. Whether it's women's beauty magazines, men's fitness titles or celebrity gossip rags, the best selling among them almost always features a happy, smiling model square and centre staring straight out at the potential reader.

It's been proven over and over that putting a recognisable face on the cover of a magazine – particularly one looking straight out towards the reader – helps it to sell, and while you might not want to put faces on the covers of each of your

Choose your pictures carefully so that they reflect not only your personality but also your writing style. Stick to portraits – creative, if you like – to avoid contravening Amazon's rules.

books, adding a personal photo to your author profile should help you connect with your readers.

Amazon lets you upload up to eight images to your account. All must be saved in Jpeg format, a minimum of 300 and a maximum of 2500 pixels in each direction, and smaller than 4MB. They should also be portrait shots, so no matter how cute you might think your cat looks wearing a Christmas hat, it won't be acceptable in your author profile.

By default your images are displayed in reverse order, so the last one you uploaded will be the one that's displayed full size on your author profile page. Either make sure you upload your headline image last, or click the *Manage* link and rearrange them.

Images are organised in reverse order, with the last picture you uploaded used as the main image on your profile. Change the order by clicking 'manage'.

Sales reports

Your basic Author Central profile is now complete. You can go on to add video and Twitter feeds if you have them, but in the interim you should explore the sales and user management features of Author Central, which let you keep a handle on live sales data. This tracks your book's performance within the Amazon catalogue in real-time.

Click the *Sales Info* tab to open your metrics, which both provides a snapshot of your book's position within Amazon's overall sales, and graphs how it has performed over time. This latter data won't be available immediately as it takes 24 hours for Amazon to add it to your Dashboard, but once it is you'll see a graph plotting your book's position over the past seven days. The closer the line runs to the top of the graph, the closer your book sits to the number one overall bestseller.

This graph needs to be read with care, however, as it doesn't necessarily reflect sales, and so can't be used to predict revenue. If your book sold 50 copies in the past week when everyone else sold 100, you'd expect to see your rank decline, even if you sold only 25 in the previous week. In this case, declining rank is masking an increase in revenue. Likewise, if you

The blue line on the sales rank graph is updated at midnight Pacific time to reflect aggregate sales; the trailing orange portion updates on the hour.

sold no copies at all, but those books that usually sold a dozen actually sold only two, you would see your rank climb over the course of seven days. In this case an improved comparative performance is not reflected in increased revenue.

To see further breakdowns of your book's performance in its specific categories you'll have to turn to its listing in Amazon's live catalogue, organised by subject category, where each book is stacked in descending order.

Your completed profile

Once completed, the public-facing side of your Author Central profile will gather together all of your books, alongside your biography and photographs. When used carefully and updated regularly it is a valuable resource that should encourage readers to buy more of your books as they become better acquainted both with you and your work.

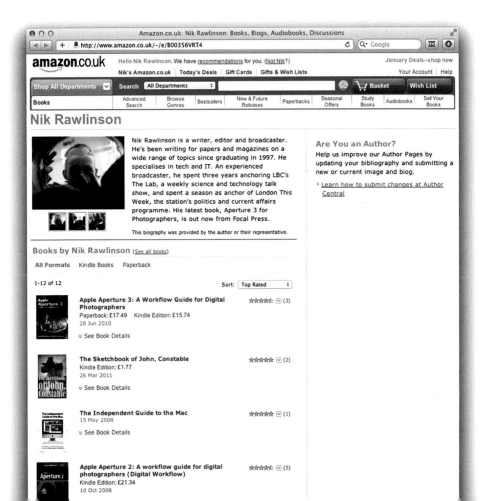

Selling books through your own site

Although Amazon and the various ePub-based digital stores are by far the biggest outlet for digital books, many writers are making a tidy living selling books through their own websites.

There are many advantages to going your own way, not least of which is the fact that you get to keep all of the proceeds yourself. As Amazon, Apple and co will be kept out of the loop they'll also be kept away from the 30% of your revenue that they'd like to pocket in exchange for listing your work in their catalogue and serving it to their customers. You'll also be paid far more quickly.

Once you've been selling books for a couple of months you'll hopefully get used to receiving regular payments from your contracted outlets, but shouldn't count on receiving anything for the first few weeks at minimum if you're selling through the Kindle Store, and longer for most aggregators submitting your work to the iBookstore and other retailers.

By selling through your own site you'll receive payments directly from your customers without the processing delay inherent in using an intermediary fulfilment service to process each sale on your behalf.

Further, you needn't comply with their formatting and pricing rules. So, it you want to sell your book in PDF format, which can be rendered on both the iPad and Kindle, but is accepted by neither the iBookstore nor Kindle Store, you can.

However, in the same way as stepping away from paid employment into the world of self-employment or freelance, there are some particular disadvantages to going your own way when it comes to digital publishing, the most obvious being that you don't have the presence and support of a recognised brand behind you. While this wouldn't be a problem for the likes of Stephen King or Dan Brown, who could sell books on the strength of their own personal brand alone, for the less-known digital publisher whose work may be unknown and who has yet to build a relationship with their readers, selling through Amazon, iBookstore or the Kobo Store offers

Selling your book through your own site means you can keep 100% of the proceeds, but you won't gain access to readers buying directly through their ereader's associated store (*above*).

Fulfilment sites like E-junkie (*bit.ly/yG95MW*) handle the complete sales process, hosting your product, processing payments and providing your customers with a download link.

their work a degree of respectability that their personal online store is unlikely to deliver.

Further, these stores, which are each directly tied to a successful hardware platform – Kindle, iPad and Kobo readers respectively – are effectively gatekeepers. Authors who choose to sell their work through such stores can be bought away from the desktop browser. This will become increasingly important over time as readers look for their next book immediately after finishing their current read, from the very device on which they consume it.

For this reason, should you wish to use a personal or business site to sell your work, we would strongly recommend doing so both by promoting existing outlets – Amazon, iBookstore and so on – for ePub and Mobipocket versions of your work, and to only directly sell alternative formats such as PDF and audiobooks through your site.

In one move you'll increase accessibility across all platforms, open up a new revenue stream and preserve your sales rank in the traditional download channels. Competing with your Amazon-hosted book on your own website will only reduce visibility by pushing your title further down Amazon's bestseller lists, reducing the chance you'll receive favourable feedback and, crucially, decreasing your visibility in lists detailing 'people who bought this book also bought...'.

Using Instant Payment Notification

Selling a book is a multi-stage process that involves advertising your product, taking payment and either manually sending the book to your customer or providing a download link from which they can retrieve it themselves. Ideally you want to offload as much of this work as possible to a third party such as E-junkie so that you can continue writing other books to sell.

E-junkie (*bit.ly/yG95MW*) provides an inexpensive shopping cart system that requires no end-user configuration or complicated coding. It will host your book on its own servers and deliver it to as many customers as choose to buy it for a flat monthly fee, handling the financial side of the transaction using Instant Payment Notification to confirm with PayPal that a payment has been received in your account before serving the download link. All you need do is design your website and embed the *Buy Now* buttons provided by E-junkie. We'll handle the web design over the page. First, you need to sign up to the service.

Signing up to E-junkie

Point your browser at *bit.ly/yG95MW* and click '*Register*'. Fill out the form to register for a free trial, and then sign in to your account. Your first week is free, after which it costs just $5 a month to host up to ten different products, with no bandwidth fees, so long as you don't consume more than 50MB of storage.

Your first task is to tell E-junkie how you want to be paid. It supports a wide range of payment processors, including Google Checkout and PayPal. In the example below we have chosen PayPal as it is one of the most widely used payment methods online, so there is a good chance that our customers will already have a PayPal account. Remember: one of your goals here is not only to make it easy for you to make sales, but also for your customers to make a purchase.

You now need to add your products to your catalogue. Submit your payment details and return to *Seller Admin*, then click *Add Product* and fill out the form. Give your product a logical name that will mean something both to

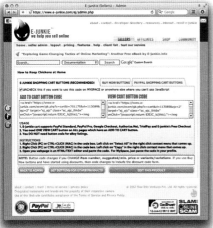

yourself and your customers and choose a price. E-junkie can handle a generous selection of currencies, including US dollars and British pounds. Select whatever is most appropriate for you, specify a price and click *Submit*. You can leave all of the other settings at their defaults (*left*).

Now you need to upload your book. Remember that to qualify for the $5-a-month account you can't exceed 50MB of storage, so make sure you have optimised any images as far as you can to reduce its file size – especially if you want to upload more books to the same account in the future. Click the *Upload Product File* button and choose the file to be uploaded.

When the upload has completed, your product is ready to sell. Copy the code from the two boxes marked *Add to cart button code* and *View cart button code*, which you'll use to embed the commerce buttons on your promotional web page (*see over*). These link directly to your product, placing it in an E-junkie hosted cart without taking your customer away from your website. You don't need to copy any graphics as these are drawn down from the E-junkie servers.

When your customers click the link to buy your book, they'll be directed to log in to your payment processor's site (PayPal, in our case), where the relevant product details and price will already be shown in the transaction details, allowing them to merely confirm the purchase. Once they do, E-junkie detects the purchase using Instant Payment Notification and emails them a link through which they can download your book while emailing you details of the sale. Your involvement in the process is nil, allowing you to watch the money arrive while you concentrate on your next writing project.

On the rare occasion that your customers need assistance – usually because the download link has expired or been binned by their spam filter – you can send them a free replacement using the E-junkie *Seller Admin* screens.

How to Publish your own eBook

Strong opening
Kick off with the book's biggest benefit, set in large type. Here, that's all you need to know to make chicken keeping fun. The secondary line drills this home if the reader was dithering: 'This eBook shows you how!'. We've included a picture of the cover of the book, which includes the title and an image bought from a photography library to reinforce the subject matter.

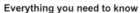

Use bullets
Lists are easier to read than blocks of running text. Break up your page with frequent use of bullet points and use CSS styles to highlight key points that will draw the eye even if your audience doesn't want to read everything.

Offer a free gift
Emulate the best-selling magazines that induce sales using free gifts. The simplest way is to create a second book containing related content. Include examples of its page layouts.

Direct purchase links
Add a purchase link after each major section, and don't forget to put one at the foot of the page to save buyers scrolling back up.

Designing your sales page

Even the most considered purchase starts with an impulse. So does every decision to close the browser window and turn away from your book. If you want to go it alone and sell your book outside of an established store, you need to grab your potential customer's attention as soon as your page hits their browser and pile on the reasons to buy until they succumb.

The key here is repetition and reinforcement.

The grab to the left shows a typical independent publication site. In common with other sites selling self-published material it is far longer than most regular informative sites, extending far below the bottom of the typical browser window. Why? Because once the vendor has attracted the potential buyer to their page they want to control the order and flow of information.

The design is intentionally old-fashioned, steering away from effects that will render in only the latest browsers to ensure the broadest possible compatibility. The exception in this instance is three points in which it uses Flash to display an interactive page-turning miniature of a selection of pages from the book. Tablet and smartphone users who may not have access to a Flash player are catered for through the inclusion of static graphics.

The colour palette is restricted to black, red and yellow, with red used to mark out sections, both as headlines and as dotted or dashed boxes around so-called 'calls to action', which include the buy buttons positioned throughout the text. There are two buy buttons on this page – one half-way down and one at the foot of the page – so that when readers reach the end of the sales pitch they only need click once to buy. That's the impulse point. If they were forced to scroll back to the top of the page you might never make that sale.

The yellow is used only to highlight key benefits and action points, such as 'healthy', 'cheap', 'easy', 'free' and 'download your books right away'. This may look garish to the design-trained eye, but that's the point: it's there to direct the reader's attention.

Finally, there's a free gift – in this instance a daily laying log book. This is positioned towards the foot of the page to reinforce the good value of the offering and convince those who are still wavering, yet sufficiently tempted to have read this far, to put their hands in their pockets. Be sure to offer something of true value here that is closely related to your core offering to avoid disappointing your audience, and don't be tempted to simply strip content from your book into a separate file. Treat your customers well and they're more likely to recommend your product to potential future readers.

Quick tips

Ensure you host your sales page on a fast server so that it loads quickly: you'll lose potential sales when customers click away if it appears too slowly. Avoid the temptation to use free, bundled web space, and always register a domain that reflects your subject matter to optimise your performance in search engine results.

Glossary

The Kindle, Kobo, Sony Reader and other digital book devices may have been designed with ease of use in mind, but they still live in a world of acronyms and jargon. To get under the skin of digital publishing, there are a few words and phrases you really ought to know, starting with these.

Adobe Digital Editions PC- and Mac-based software used to manage digital books and synchronise them with several hardware ereaders. It features strong digital rights tools, allowing publishers to protect their work and public libraries to use it as a means of lending books for a limited period.

Bookmark As with regular printed publications, a marker used to keep track of a particular place in a digital book. It is usually possible to set several bookmarks in a single publication and save them so that they can later be used as reference sources. In reality, its closest analogue equivalent is turning down the corner of a printed page.

Calibre eBook management tool used to catalogue and convert between formats.

Compression When images on a website or embedded in a digital book are made smaller so that they either download more quickly or take up less space in the device's memory, they are said to have been compressed. Compression involves selectively removing parts of the file that are less easily seen or heard by the human eye and ear, and simplifying the more complex parts.

Digital Rights Management (DRM) Additional encoded data added to a digitised piece of audio or video or, of most interest to us, a book. DRM controls the way in which it will work, usually preventing it from being shared among several users.

e-ink Screen technology used in all Kindles except for the Kindle Fire. Also used by the Kobo Touch and Wireless, Sony Reader and others. Uses reflected light rather than being backlit and so is often easier to read in bright light than an LCD equivalent. Currently monochrome, but colour editions are being developed.

Encoding The process of capturing an analogue data source, such as an image, and translating it into a digital format. Although files can be encoded with no loss of quality, the process usually also involves compression to reduce file sizes.

ePub (Electronic PUBlication) An open eBook format developed by the International Digital Publishing Forum. As it is free to implement it is well supported and used as the preferred file format of many ereaders, including Sony Reader, the Kobo readers and Apple's iBooks app. It is incompatible with current models of the Amazon Kindle.

Fairplay Digital Rights Management mechanism used to protect books sold through the Apple iBookstore. Also used for other content bought through the iTunes Store such as films, TV shows and some music downloads, although restrictions on the latter have been slightly relaxed over time.

Firmware Operating system built into a device such as a hardware eBook reader that controls all of its core functions. The closest equivalent in a regular computer is the operating system that hosts the various applications it runs. Windows, Linux and Mac OS X are three examples. Amazon has released the source code for the Kindle's operating system so that it can be downloaded and examined by the general public, and also delivers periodic updates that add new features to its devices. Apple has not released the source code to iBooks, its own reader app for the iPhone, iPad and iPod touch.

GB Gigabyte. One billion bytes, and a means of measuring the capacity of a device or the size of a file. A byte is made up of eight bits, and a bit is equivalent to a single character, such as a, b, c, 4, 5, 6 and so on. As digital files are encoded using the characters 0 and 1, each digit that makes up part of its encoding will represent one bit, every eight characters will make one byte, every 1,024 bytes will equal a kilobyte and every million kilobytes will equate to a gigabyte (allowing for rounding).

Home Screen The term used to describe the screen within the various ereader interfaces that displays the icons or links for the various downloaded books and other media content.

HTML Acronym for HyperText Mark-up Language, the code used to program web pages and underpinning much of the ePub format. It is a plain-English language code, which uses simple tags such as <b> to denote bold, <i> to instigate italics and <p> to mark the start of a paragraph. Several applications, such as Adobe Dreamweaver, greatly simplify the task of writing web pages by allowing programmers to work in a desktop publishing-style layout mode, rather than having to manipulate raw code. HTML is often supplemented by attached styling information in the form of Cascading Style Sheets (CSS). Browsers combine the two to construct a page.

InDesign Page-layout application from Adobe that has latterly adopted many digital publishing tools for creating eBooks and interactive magazines.

Kindle Line of successful digital ereading devices developed by Lab126, a Cupertino-based internal department of Internet book retailer Amazon.

Kindle Format 8 (KF8) Proposed replacement for Mobi 7 (see *Mobipocket*, below) that allows for more flexible publishing to Amazon Kindle devices by introducing 150 new formatting capabilities. These include more complex tables, a wider choice of graphics types, floating elements, drop capitals and fixed layouts that will allow publishers to more closely replicate their print-based publications in digital form. It is underpinned by support for HTML5 and CSS3, bringing it much closer to the ePub format used by the Kindle's main rivals.

Mobipocket The name of both a French company and the eBook reader software it produces. The Mobipocket software is the basis of the format used by Amazon for publishing and rendering eBooks on the Kindle. The company was acquired by Amazon in 2005.

QuarkXPress Long-standing page-layout suite developed by Quark, which was once the defacto choice for designing magazines and newspapers. It now shares that task with InDesign. Later revisions have introduced fully-fledged eBook and digital magazine publishing workflows.

Sync Short for synchronise. The means of swapping data and purchases between the Kindle and Amazon's network. Traditionally performed using Amazon's Whispersync technology, although you can also transfer content manually by connecting your Kindle to your computer and dragging it across.

USB Universal Serial Bus. A socket, plug and cable system that allows almost any peripheral to be connected to a Mac or PC, including printers, mice, keyboards and so on. The Kindle also uses USB as a means of exchanging media content with a computer when connected physically and, now that Amazon is not shipping power plugs with most of its Kindle products, it is also a connection through which you can charge your device.

Whispernet Virtual network used by Amazon to manage the passage of data to, from and between Kindles, Kindle applications and user accounts.

Whispersync Amazon's name for the process of keeping each of the books you are reading updated with your current page, bookmarks, notes and so on, across multiple devices or Kindle reading applications.